Dishes
and
Devotions

by Tammi Arender

MICHTER HOUSE
PUBLISHING
an imprint of
Rope Swing Publishing

ISBN: 978-1-964026-22-0 (paperback)
ISBN: 978-1-964026-23-7 (hardback)

Acknowledgments

First, to my family. My sister Cynthia Arender Machen, her children and grandchildren have been the light of my life.

My sister-in-law Penney Wilkins and her children and grandchildren, whom I've not spent nearly enough time with.

My brother Stan Wilkins, cousins Lori Joyner and Alan Williamson and those who've put up with my crazy over the years.

My "Round Away Road" neighbor Bill Windham and his wife Carol. I never would have started the arduous process of putting the stories and recipes on paper if you had not allowed me to hold up in your private getaway, undisturbed, for several days.

Rope Swing Publishing, and their teams, who believed in this project from the start.

Thank you all for listening to my stories and sharing my love of food and Jesus!

"Taste and see that the Lord is good" Psalm 34:8

Introduction

Food is my love language. It was my dad's love language. If you came to our house when I was a kid, it was a tasty visit. If Daddy wasn't out on the tractor or combine on our farm, he was usually in the kitchen. Billy Ray Arender wanted to tickle your taste buds and tickle your funny bone. In this cookbook, I hope to do the same. With God's help, my daddy's affection for food, my love for Jesus and my culinary curiosity, I aim to help you make every day delicious!

I grew up in Louisiana, so I often say, "I came out of the womb knowing how to cook!" But that's really not the case. I was such a tomboy that I didn't spend much time in the kitchen. Now don't get me wrong, I never missed a meal! I weighed 170 pounds in the eighth grade! But I do regret not spending more time at the edge of my dad and my grandmother's aprons. Now there was a cook! Effie Mae Prewitt, my mom's mom. We called her Ma-mae, short for Mama Mae. I fondly remember her Caramel Cake, Rum Cake and her pancakes. Those pancakes were perfection on a plate. I remember begging to spend the night at Mamae's on Friday nights so I could wake up to those pancakes and cartoons on Saturday mornings! That was better than a trip to Disney World! To this day, I can't get my pancakes to look or taste like hers. Her batter was the best. I believe she used buttermilk. But it was those crispy charred edges that she got on them that I can't duplicate. It was like a ring of caramelized goodness that encased those buttery, melt in your mouth flapjacks. You almost didn't need syrup! So let's start with those Mae Prewitt pancakes.

Mamae's Pancakes

2 cups all-purpose flour
3 Tbsp granulated sugar
1 tsp baking soda
½ tsp baking powder
¼ tsp salt
2 cups whole buttermilk
½ cup unsalted butter, melted and cooled
2 large eggs
1½ tsp vanilla extract
Butter for pan
Ribbon cane syrup (or your favorite syrup, but we always use ribbon cane) for serving

Start by combining the flour, sugar, baking powder, and baking soda together in a bowl. Mix buttermilk, butter, eggs, and vanilla together in another bowl; add the flour mixture. Mamae always used a cast iron skillet. Put the butter in the skillet and turn up the heat to medium-high heat. Spoon or pour ⅓ to ½ cup of batter into the skillet. Cook pancakes until bubbles appear. And the edges are golden brown and crispy. Using a large spatula, flip pancakes. Cook until golden brown.

Add-ons: Over the years I started adding toasted pecans or bananas to my pancakes. I also loved to add a ½ cup of pureed sweet potatoes and cinnamon to my batter. You'll learn I add sweet potatoes to lots of my dishes!

Tammi's Tips: Use a cast iron Skillet

Don't overmix the batter. As a matter of fact, even leave a few "lumps" in the batter. That's okay. Better not to overmix.

Rest the batter for a few minutes before cooking.

Other dishes from my grandmother's kitchen as found in the Brushy Bayou Cookbook:

Caramel Cake

Cake:
1 cup butter, room temperature
2 cups sugar
4 large eggs, room temperature
3 cups self-rising flour
1 cup buttermilk, room temperature
2 tsp vanilla

Icing:
2 cups sugar
1 cup buttermilk
½ cup Crisco
½ cup butter
1 tsp baking soda

Cake:

Preheat oven to 350° F. I go ahead and prep three 9 cake pans and cover them with butter and flour. (I have used the cooking spray with flour in it, and it works well). Set aside.

Put the butter and sugar into the bowl of a stand mixer. Cream together for a minute or two. Add the eggs one at a time. Then, you alternate adding the flour and buttermilk, ending with the flour.

Pour the batter into your prepared pans. If you want to be really precise so the layers are even, I suggest using a digital scale. You'll bake until the center springs back to a light touch or a toothpick comes out clean. Cook for 25 to 30 minutes depending on your oven. Keep a close eye on it in the last five minutes. Do not over bake.

Allow the cakes to cool for about 5 minutes and then turn them out onto wire racks to cool completely.

Icing:

Mix all ingredients in a 3 or 4 quart heavy-bottom pan or cast iron Dutch oven. Put it over medium heat.

Don't stir but swirl the pan to keep ingredients moving but not splattering sugar crystals.

Now you'll need your candy thermometer. I know my grandmother didn't use one because she could "eyeball" it. I can't do that. Cook to softball stage 235-245°F on a candy thermometer.

And this is where it's almost like making pralines. You remove from heat and beat with a wooden spoon until creamy and ready to spread. You could also do this in a mixer if you prefer. But there's something magical about doing by hand with that wooden spoon.

Rum Cake

Cake:
3⅔ cups cake flour
1½ tsp baking powder
¾ tsp salt
2 cups granulated sugar
¾ cup unsalted butter, softened
¼ cup vegetable oil
3 large eggs, room temperature
2 egg yolks, room temperature
2 tsp vanilla extract
¾ cup dark rum
½ cup whole milk

Glaze:
6 tbsp unsalted butter
½ cup granulated sugar
2 Tbsp water
pinch of salt
¼ cup dark rum

Cake: First, preheat the oven to 325°F.

In a medium bowl, sift together the flour, salt, and baking powder.

In the bowl of your stand mixer (or you can use a handheld mixer as well), beat the sugar, butter, and oil on medium speed. You want this to become light and fluffy. It takes about 5 minutes. Add the eggs and egg yolks, one at a time. Finally, add vanilla, beating just until combined. Don't overmix.

It's important to stir together the rum and whole milk. You'll alternate the dry ingredients with the rum/milk mixture. End with the flour mixture.

I use a Bundt pan. Butter and flour it. Pour the batter into pan. Gently drop the pan on the counter a couple of times to settle the batter. Bake for 1 hour or until a wooden pick inserted in the center comes out clean.

Glaze: Melt the butter in a small saucepan (heavy bottom preferred, so it cooks more evenly) over medium heat. Add the sugar, water, and salt, stirring until fully combined. Bring to a boil, about 2 minutes.

Stir in the rum. Continue boiling, stirring occasionally until the sauce starts to thicken. This takes about 2 to 3 minutes. Remove from the heat. Transfer the mixture to a heat-proof bowl.

When the cake is ready, poke holes all over the bottom of the cake using a skewer. (My grandmother used to let me do this!) Pour half of the rum sauce over the cake, letting it soak in for 15 minutes.

Then invert the cake onto a cake plate or whatever you're serving it on. Spoon or brush the remaining glaze over the warm cake.

Tammi's tips for the best cake: Measure your flour. I like to spoon my flour into the measuring cup. But the most accurate way to measure flour is by using a kitchen scale.

Separate the eggs while cold. Eggs are easier to separate while they are still cold, so do this right when you take the eggs out of the fridge. But let them come to room temp before assembling the cake batter.

Daddy Could Make Dirt Sing

My daddy knew the way to my heart was through my stomach. We ate pretty much from his garden. And wow, could that man grow some goodies! I swear he could grow stuff out of concrete. Other farmers throughout Madison Parish would want to come just to touch Daddy's arm or shirt sleeve just to see if any of his crop-growing mojo would rub off on them!

"I remember when Billy Ray would come to the seed store and he would sit in his truck and wait on the warehouse guys to bring out his soybean seed. Other farmers would run outside to say hello and 'accidentally on purpose' touch Billy Ray's arm through his lowered window of his truck. They knew he could grow soybeans or a garden when everyone else was struggling. That man was a farmer's farmer," said Malcolm Bishop, Sanders Seed Company, Tallulah, Louisiana.

When I heard the story from my daddy's friend Malcolm Bishop about how young farmers in the area, just wanted to touch my father's shirtsleeve, hoping some of his farming intuition would rub off on them, it reminded me of the woman who wanted to touch the hem of Jesus' garment. You remember that story in the book of Mark? This woman had been sick with "female issues" for 26 years. Being a woman, I can't even imagine! But she had such faith that she knew if she just got close to Jesus and touched the hem of his robe, she would be healed!

I know my dad had no healing powers. He certainly couldn't snap his fingers and make plants grow. But he did have talent and a farming instinct that not everyone had. He actually had only a fourth-grade education. But he had a truckload of common sense. I hope that we all can learn from this. That if we get close to Jesus, through His word, through prayer, through fellowship with other believers, we can walk away healed. We can walk in the confidence and knowledge that we can do all things through Jesus. Just believe and each day try to "touch the hem of his garment!"

Let's get back to the garden. If you're a country girl like me, chances are you've eaten butter beans, purple hull peas, collard greens, turnip greens, carrots and tomatoes fresh from the garden.

I didn't know how good that was until I moved away to college. It was just 50 miles down the road in Monroe, Louisiana, but it still took me far away from that fresh from the garden goodness and put me way to close to Johnny's Pizza and their famous "Sweep the Kitchen!" I didn't put on the freshman 20, I put on the freshman 40! It's also where I got introduced to carbs. I didn't know carbs were my enemy. Or that I was supposed to count them! We didn't eat a lot of bread with our meals on the farm unless it was cornbread.

Then, I moved to Baton Rouge, Louisiana, to go to work at WBRZ. That was more than three hours away from Daddy's cookin'. But some of my fondest memories were coming home to Tallulah from Baton Rouge, and Daddy would time it just right. He'd have me a perfectly cooked steak and a skillet full of fried potatoes. And I mean those potatoes were a party in my mouth (So I guess I did know what a carb was—because I ate my weight in those "hashbrown" potatoes!) Daddy had this knack for getting them crispy on the outside and soft as butter on the inside. And he cooked them in a cast iron skillet the size of a hubcap on his truck!

Southern Fried Potatoes

4 large russet or Yukon gold potatoes, scrubbed and cut into ¾-inch chunks
1 small onion, diced (optional but traditional)
3 Tbsp bacon grease (or butter, or vegetable oil)
1 tsp salt, divided
½ tsp black pepper
¼ tsp garlic powder

Place potato chunks in a pot of salted water. Bring to a boil and cook 5 to 7 minutes, until just fork-tender. Drain well and let them dry completely. In a large cast iron skillet, heat bacon grease or oil over medium-high heat until shimmering. Add the potatoes: Spread potatoes in a single layer. Sprinkle with ½ tsp salt and black pepper. Cook without stirring for 5 to 7 minutes, until the bottoms are golden brown and crispy. Flip and season: Gently turn potatoes with a spatula. Add onions and garlic powder. Continue cooking, stirring occasionally, for another 10 to 15 minutes, until evenly browned and tender.

Tammi's Tips for Southern Fried Potatoes:
Use a cast iron skillet. Use Russett potatoes. Don't rush them. Resist the temptation to start flipping them before they've truly formed a crust on the bottom. Chop the potato cubes to consistent sizes. Use vegetable oil, not nonstick cooking spray.

Devotion

So many of us are walking through life carrying wounds no one sees. Some are physical, but so many more are emotional, spiritual, or buried deep in places we do not talk about. This woman in Scripture did not just need a physical healing. She needed hope, connection, and restoration of dignity. She had been isolated, overlooked, and dismissed for so long that just getting close enough to touch Jesus felt like a miracle in itself. Some of us have been carrying private pain for years too, and we have forgotten what it feels like to expect healing.

Notice also that she did not need a full audience with Jesus. She did not need permission or proof that she qualified. She simply needed to reach. A single touch was enough. Your faith, even in its smallest and most fragile form, is enough to move heaven closer to you. Jesus still responds to the reaching heart.

If you are tired, hurting, or unsure of what tomorrow holds, your step of faith may be as small as whispering His name. Healing does not always come instantly or visibly, but the moment you reach for Him, your story changes direction. When God steps into your weakness, He becomes the strength you cannot manufacture on your own. Just as the woman wanted a little of your daddy's gift to rub off on her, we can come close to the true source and let His presence rub off on us. His peace, His strength, and His healing.

SCRIPTURE (NIV):
"When she heard about Jesus, she came up behind him in the crowd and touched his cloak, because she thought, 'If I just touch his clothes, I will be healed.' Immediately her bleeding stopped, and she felt in her body that she was freed from her suffering." — Mark 5:27–29

PRAYER:
Lord, help me remember that I do not have to have all the answers. I have only to reach for You. Draw my heart close to Yours and heal the places in me that no one else sees. Give me the courage to come near, the faith to believe, and the peace that comes from knowing You are still my healer. Amen.

Scattered and Fried

They should put me on the menu at Waffle House! Because I'm tough as Waffle House steak and as scattered and fried as their hashbrowns! Sometimes don't you just feel like a plate of hash browns? Scattered and fried, smothered and covered? You feel like life is laughing at you. You can barely keep your nose above the waterline. You want to scream for a 'time out' but your screams aren't heard. Everyone else is screaming too!

These days you're smothered and covered on your days off, just like your workdays. You want to go to Zumba, Spin, or Pilates, but carving an hour out of your day is like carving a pumpkin made out of granite. You know our grandparents didn't go to "cardio" or have to count carbs and calories. They worked out in the gym of life. They rested on Sundays. They ate their meals with their kids around a table. Not in a car seat of an SUV with happy meals and a built-in DVD.

We live in the most cutting-edge technological time in history. But those advances push us to our limits of connecting, creating, and conforming. We don't know how to "be" in the moment with the people who mean the most to us. I say order up some family time and some face time. I don't mean on your smartphone either. I mean, get reacquainted with the dining room table and look at each other. Play a game of "highlight"/"lowlight". Go around the table and tell the high point of your day and the low point of your day. And listen, really listen. Make the dinner table a phone-free zone. Don't spend another day feeling like a plate of hashbrowns! It's your day to be sunny-side up! Order up! (ding ding)

Pan Seared Rib-eye

1 sirloin steak
salt and pepper to taste,
1 tbsp Worcestershire sauce
1 tbsp butter
2 cloves of garlic minced

This is the stovetop method for cooking the perfect steak. 'Cause that's what Daddy did. You can use the marinade of your choice; Daddy just used Worcestershire.

Tammi's tips for the best steak: Do not put salt and pepper on it first. Pepper, specifically will scorch in the hot pan. Salt will dry out the meat. Save the salt and pepper for last. Same with garlic. Garlic burns easily, so it's best to wait.

Preheat the cast iron skillet. Almost to the point of smoking hot. Then, place a tablespoonof butter in the skillet. After a few minutes on each side for searing, lower the heat to medium. Now, if you like your steak rare (like I do, my sister actually likes hers still mooing!) you may only have to cook it another minute or so on the lower heat. You should also tilt the pan and baste the steak with the butter and juices.

Remove the steak from pan and let it rest for 10 minutes. Now you can add salt and pepper to taste.

Turnip Greens

1 tbsp unsalted butter
½ lb bacon
1 cup yellow onions, diced
½ cup red bell pepper, diced
1 Tbsp garlic, minced
2½ cups chicken broth
1 ham hock
sea salt & cracked black pepper to taste
2½ lb turnips greens, washed and cut
½ tsp baking soda

In a large pot fry up the bacon. Remove the bacon after done and leave the grease. Add the butter. Add onions and red peppers and cook until tender. Add garlic. Cook garlic until it smells so good you could it just this! Add chicken broth and ham hock. Let broth simmer for 10 minutes. Add turnips greens to pot. Stir, cover and cook on low for 1 hour (stirring and checking on them occasionally). Remove lid and taste to adjust seasonings again. If you like yours spicy (I don't) add red pepper flakes or tobacco. Some southern folks also add liquid smoke. But I don't ever have that on hand, so I don't. Cover and simmer for an additional 10 to 20 minutes or until greens are tender to your liking.

Devotion

There is something sacred about the way a garden connects us back to what is simple and good. Long before we knew anything about carbs, sugar counts, or calorie charts, we knew what it felt like to eat what came straight from the ground, still warm from the sun. There is a kind of nourishment that goes deeper than the body, because it carries memory, care, and love from the hands that prepared it.

When I think about those homecomings and Daddy waiting with a skillet full of fried potatoes and a steak timed to perfection, I am reminded of the way God welcomes us back when we have wandered far from where our soul feels fed. We might not even realize we are starving until we taste home again. The world offers convenience, quick satisfaction, and noisy substitutes, but it can never replace the nourishment that comes from being near the One who tends our hearts the way a farmer tends a field.

Sometimes we drift without meaning to. Life pulls us into busyness, distraction, and distance from the simple closeness we once had with God. Yet He keeps the "meal" hot, waiting for our return… not with punishment or shame, but with the warmth of love that says, I knew you would come home. Just like a well-tended garden keeps producing for the one who planted it, God keeps producing grace for the one who returns, even after seasons away.

SCRIPTURE (NIV):
"Yet the LORD longs to be gracious to you; therefore he will rise up to show you compassion. For the LORD is a God of justice. Blessed are all who wait for him!"
— Isaiah 30:18

PRAYER:
Father, draw my heart back to the place where I am nourished by You. Help me recognize when I have settled for less than what brings life to my soul. Thank You for always keeping the door open, the table warm, and the welcome steady. Teach me to return to You daily, to taste and see Your goodness again and again. Amen.

Cornbread Dressing

Cornbread:
1 cup self-rising cornmeal (I use Martha White)
½ cup self-rising flour (I use White Lily)
¾ cup whole buttermilk
2 eggs
2 tbsp vegetable oil

Dressing:
8 Tbsp butter (1 stick)
3 medium onion chopped
4 stalks celery chopped
1½ tsp dried sage
1 tsp poultry seasoning
¾ tsp salt
½ tsp pepper
½ cup milk
3 hard-boiled eggs
2-to-2½ cups chicken stock or broth
2 Tbsp butter

Start by making your cornbread a couple of days in advance. (It is better when it's a little dried out). To make the cornbread: Preheat oven to 400°F. Put your cast iron skillet that you're using for your cornbread (I use an 8") in the oven while it's preheating. Put in a tablespoon of shortening.

In a medium bowl, stir together all the ingredients for cornbread. Pour batter into your hot cast iron skillet. Bake for 20 to 25 minutes. When ready to make the dressing, crumble the cornbread into small pieces.

Now for the dressing. Melt butter over medium heat in a large pan. Add your chopped celery and onion. Cook until tender. Add sage, poultry seasoning, salt, and pepper to onion mixture. Put your crumbled cornbread in a large bowl. Add hard-boiled eggs to your bowl of crumbled cornbread. Then, stir in 2 cups of chicken broth. Stir in onion mixture. Mixture should be very moist. Add more broth if necessary. Transfer to a greased baking dish. Cut butter into small slivers and scatter on top of dressing. Bake at 350°F for 30 minutes, or until it turns light brown on top.

Tammi's tips for perfect hard-boiled eggs: I love a good deviled egg! My grandmother put hard-boiled eggs in her dressing. And I loved it. So this takes the guesswork out of making the perfect hard-boiled egg. Put your desired number of eggs in a pot and cover with cold water to cover. Turn the heat on high. When water starts to boil, turn off heat, cover the pan with a lid. Let stand for 17 minutes. Don't lift the lid! Pour out the hot water and pour cold water over the eggs. Let stand for another 20 minutes or longer. When ready to peel, run under cold water. It makes the shells come off easier!

The Process and Reward

As I mentioned, I grew up not really knowing I needed to count carbs. I knew I liked bread, rice, spaghetti, and anything fried. So you can imagine my horror when the whole "Atkins" diet came along and we were told we could only have like 10 carbs in one day. I have 10 carbs before I finish breakfast!! I have managed to cut back on my carb intake, since my slow-as-a-snail metabolism requires it, but I still love a good yeast roll. As a matter of fact, bread is how my baking obsession got started. Let me take you back to that cold, rainy day in Baton Rouge when the baking "light bulb" went off in my head.

I'm an outdoors girl. I love riding horses, Harleys and hiking along any trail or in a park. If it's 55 degrees or above, I'm walking and being Dora the Explorer. But on a cold, wet December day in Baton Rouge many years ago, I was stuck inside. Normally being stuck inside on a late fall weekend wouldn't be a problem because I'm also a college football and NFL fan. So, my beloved LSU Tigers and my New Orleans Saints would probably be playing. Bringing back memories of tailgating with my cousin Alan Williamson and his buddies. Also, James and Justin Peck, who always had amazing gatherings just outside Tiger Stadium in Baton Rouge. Many times, I just went to the games for the tailgating food and never went to the game!! (Remind me to add a chapter about tailgating foods.) But back to my story. At this point in the season, neither of my teams made the playoffs. I was forced to watch teams I cared nothing about.

So with nasty weather and no football to watch, I decided to try my hand at making homemade yeast bread. I was craving my grandmother's melt in your mouth rolls. I thought, "How hard can it be?" So, I found one of my mother's old cookbooks and landed on homemade bread. The kind you knead by hand, let rise twice, rolls. And guess what? They turned out fabulous! I was shocked. That sparked the baking bug in me. I figured if I could follow a recipe, then maybe I could do more fancy-schmancy dishes. I started reading those cookbooks like John Grisham novels! Then my dear cousin, Lori Joyner, started gifting me cookbooks for Christmas and birthdays. From that day on, if I had a craving for something, instead of going to a restaurant or a store, I picked up a cookbook and made it from scratch. I learned I liked the process of cooking and baking as much as I liked the reward of eating it.

John 6:35 Jesus said, "I am the bread of life. Whoever comes to me will never go hungry. Whoever believes in me will never be thirsty."

Devotion

It takes heat, and often more than we think we can bear, to make something special. No one enjoys being in the hot seat. We shift, we squirm, and we look for relief as quickly as possible. Yet some of the best things we enjoy today are only formed because they endured the fire.

Think about the difference between a raw egg and a cooked one. Other than Rocky Balboa, who famously gulped down raw eggs for training, most of us would rather have them transformed into something warm and delicious. Whether sunny-side up, scrambled, poached or turned into deviled eggs, the egg does not become enjoyable without time in the heat. You cannot simply sit it beside the boiling water and expect transformation. It must go through the heat for the change to take place.

The same is true for gold. It is beautiful when refined, but before it shines, it is put into the fire to remove what does not belong. Only after the impurities are melted away does its full worth become visible.

When God allows us to sit in seasons of heat, pressure, or discomfort, He is not trying to destroy us. He is purifying us. He is making us stronger, wiser, and more like Him. The heat reveals what needs to be surrendered. It surfaces the things we did not see, or maybe did not want to see, so that God can refine them by His grace. We want to run from the fire, but sometimes the greatest transformation happens when we stay with Him in it.

If you feel pressed on every side today, pause for a moment. Ask the Lord what He is refining in you. The heat is not a punishment; it is a preparation. The fire that feels fierce today might be the very thing shaping you into a vessel He can trust with greater purpose tomorrow. You will not stay in the furnace forever. But you will not come out the same as you went in. You will come out shining.

SCRIPTURE (NIV) :
"So that the proven character of your faith—more precious than gold, which perishes even though refined by fire—may result in praise, glory, and honor at the revelation of Jesus Christ."
—1 Peter 1:7

PRAYER:
Father, I thank You for standing with me even when the fire feels hot, and the pressure feels heavy. Remind me that You are not harming me, but refining me. Help me release anything in my heart that does not reflect You. Strengthen my faith so that I may come through this season purified, not discouraged. Teach me to trust Your process and lean on Your presence. Let this refining produce a deeper confidence in You, a steadier peace in my spirit, and a heart that reflects Your character more each day. In Jesus' name, Amen.

Yeast Bread (or rolls)

2 ½ cups whole or 2% milk, warmed to 80-100°F
1 Tbsp active dry yeast
2 Tbsp granulated sugar
4 Tbsp (½ stick) butter, melted and cooled to room temperature
6 cups all-purpose flour (or bread flour)
1 Tbsp salt

Start by combining the warmed milk, yeast and sugar to the bowl of your stand mixer and whisk together (when I did this the first time I didn't own a stand mixer, so I did it all by hand!) Let it rest for about 5 minutes, until the yeast is activated and foamy. Whisk in the melted butter.

If you have a dough hook for your mixer, use it. Add 4 cups of flour to the milk and yeast mixture. Turn the mixer to low and start to bring the dough together. If doing this behind, I suggest using a wooden spoon to bring the dough together. This isn't the kneading process. That comes later. Slowly add enough flour to bring the dough together into a soft, smooth dough. The dough should clean the sides of the bowl, but still stick slightly to the bottom.

Continue kneading the dough, slowly sprinkling in the salt. Once the salt is incorporated, let the mixer continue to knead the dough for another 5 minutes, until the dough is elastic, smooth and soft.

Now you'll transfer the dough ball to a greased bowl large enough to hold double the amount of dough. Cover the bowl with plastic wrap or a dish towel.

Let the dough rest at room temperature until it has doubled in size. Depending on the temperature of the room, this will take between 45 minutes and 1.5 hours.

Grease or spray two 8.5x4.5" loaf pans with non-stick spray, or coat with a bit of melted butter. Dump the dough out onto a clean work surface and divide into two pieces. Lift one piece of dough and form it into a ball. Lay the ball of dough on your work surface, and roll it back and forth a few times to create an oblong ball. Lay the dough, seam side down, into one of the loaf pans. Repeat with the other half of dough.

Again, cover each loaf with a dish towel or plastic wrap.

Allow the loaves to rise at room temperature until they double in size again, rising over the tops of the pans, 45 minutes to 1.5 hours.

Preheat your oven to 375°F. When the loaves are fully risen, bake for 35 to 45 minutes, until they are golden brown and an instant-read thermometer put into the center of one of the loaves registers 190-200°F.

Remove from the oven and lift each loaf and place it onto a wire rack. Allow to cool completely.

Cranberry Bread

⅓ cup orange juice
zest of one large orange
⅔ cup buttermilk
6 Tbsp unsalted butter, melted
1 large egg
2 cups all-purpose flour
1 cup granulated sugar
1 tsp iodized salt
1 tsp baking powder
¼ tsp baking soda
1½ cups (6 oz) cranberries, coarsely chopped
½ cup chopped walnuts

Grease a 9x5" loaf pan with butter or shortening. I like to use shortening. Then preheat oven to 375°F.

Start by stirring together the orange juice, orange zest, buttermilk, butter, and egg.

In a separate bowl, whisk together the flour, sugar, salt, baking powder, and baking soda. Stir in the wet ingredients, mixing until just combined.

Stir in the chopped cranberries and nuts, if using.

Pour the batter into the prepared loaf pan and bake for 25 minutes, then reduce heat to 350° Fahrenheit and bake for an additional 45 to 50 minutes. Cool in the pan for 10 minutes, then transfer to a wire rack and let cool at least an additional 30 minutes before slicing.

Devotion

I think one of my biggest life lessons came from the kitchen. How little things can have big impacts. Just a tablespoon of yeast can turn large amounts of flour and water into a huge loaf of bread. So many times we think we have to be another Billy Graham, Mother Theresa or Corrie Ten Boom to have an impact. But it's the little things, a kind word, a text, a phone call, a letter, an offer to babysit, cook a meal or run errands that can make a difference in someone's day. Be mindful of those around you who may just need a little encouragement. Be the "yeast" and help someone's spirits rise today!

The truth is, our souls know the difference between being filled and being merely entertained. Just like food from a garden tastes richer because it came from real soil and slow growth, a life rooted in God carries a deeper flavor than anything the world can season for a moment and then snatch away. We were made for that kind of goodness; the kind that does not come from shortcuts, but from staying close to the One who cultivates life in us.

Maybe you have been living off quick spiritual snacks without realizing it. Maybe your heart has been nibbling on encouragement one day and discouragement the next, never quite satisfied, never quite full. God has more for you than survival. He invites you to come back to a table that has been prepared with patience, tenderness, and love… the same way someone who loves you would season and fry potatoes in a cast iron skillet waiting for you to walk through the door.

When you feel worn out or spiritually hungry, that dissatisfaction is not failure, it is a holy reminder that you belong somewhere richer, somewhere rooted, somewhere real. God does not scold you for feeling empty. He simply says, Come sit with Me again. Let Me feed your spirit. Let Me restore what distance has drained.

This is the beauty of God's love: there is always another plate, another welcome, another serving of grace waiting. You are never too far gone, never too empty, and never too late to return to the place where your soul is fed again.

SCRIPTURE (NIV):
"Taste and see that the Lord is good; blessed is the one who takes refuge in Him." — Psalm 34:8

"A little yeast works through a whole batch of dough."
—Galatians 5:9

PRAYER: Father, thank You for nourishing me in ways the world never can. Bring me back to You whenever I drift,and teach me to recognize the hunger in my soul as an invitation to return to Your presence. Fill me with Your goodness until my spirit is satisfied again. Amen.

Pumpkin Swirl Bread

1 (8 oz) package cream cheese (softened)
¼ cup white sugar
1 egg, beaten
1¾ cups all-purpose flour
1½ cups white sugar
1 tsp baking soda
1 tsp ground cinnamon
½ tsp salt
¼ tsp ground nutmeg
1 cup pumpkin puree (or sweet potato puree)
½ cup butter, melted
1 egg, beaten
⅓ cup milk
1 tsp vanilla

Blend cream cheese, ¼ cup sugar, 1 tsp vanilla and 1 beaten egg. Set aside.

Combine flour, 1½ cups white sugar, baking soda, salt, and spices. Set aside.

Combine pumpkin, butter or margarine, beaten egg, and milk. Add flour mixture to pumpkin mixture, mixing just until moistened. Reserve 2 cups of the pumpkin batter. Pour the remaining batter into a greased and floured 9x5" loaf pan. Pour cream cheese mixture over pumpkin batter, and top with reserved pumpkin batter. Cut through batter several times with a knife for a swirl effect.

Bake at 350°F for 70 minutes, or until tester comes out clean. Cool in the pan for 10 minutes, and then remove from pan to cool completely.

Let me stop right here and tell you a funny about my Pumpkin Swirl Bread. I worked for about 10 minutes as a news anchor at WOWK TV in Charleston, West Virginia. One weekend I told my co-anchor that I was going to make pumpkin swirl bread. I noticed his face sort scrunched up, and he forced a smile and squeezed out the words, "I can't wait to try it." The next day I came in with my pretty pumpkin swirl bread, and he said he was reluctant to try it because he'd never had anything made with squirrel. I said, squirrel?! He thought I said pumpkin 'squirrel' bread! I guess he had heard a few of my stories of growing up in the country and my daddy shooting anything that ran across the yard, skinning it and putting it in a skillet and we'd eat it. Heck, we knew if you cover it with enough gravy and/or ketchup, you call it supper! So he thought maybe that's normal for them country folk!

Sweet Potato Bread Pudding with Praline Sauce

Pudding:

8-9 cups of soft white bread
 (I make my own yeast bread
 but can use challah or brioche)
1 cup heavy whipping cream
½ cup whole milk
½ cup sugar
1 large egg and 3 yolks
½ tsp salt
1 tsp vanilla
1 tsp ground cinnamon
½ tsp ground ginger
½ tsp ground nutmeg
1½ sticks melted butter
½ cup high-quality chocolate chips
1 cup pureed sweet potato

Sauce:
½ cup light brown sugar
½ cup heavy cream
¼ cup butter
1 cup pecans
2 tsp vanilla

Pudding:

Melt half a stick of butter in glass 9x13" baking dish in 350°F oven. If bread has a "crust" remove crust. Pull bread apart into bite size pieces. Place bread into dish with melted butter. Melt the other stick of butter and pour over bread trying to cover all pieces. Let sit and soak up butter while making sweet potato/cream bath.

Puree sweet potato in mini food process with 1 Tbsp of butter and 1 Tbsp of molasses. In another bowl, whisk together all other ingredients then whisk in pureed sweet potato. Pour over buttered bread mixture. Sprinkle in white chocolate chips. Press down white chocolate chips and bread into cream bath. Making sure all bread is submerged. If bread isn't originally soft and doughy, it needs to sit for about 20 minutes to soak up cream mixture. The softer the bread, the less time it takes.

Place dish in a water bath in oven for 30 to 35 minutes. When bread pudding is done let it sit for a few minutes before cutting.

Sauce:

Mix brown sugar and butter in a saucepan on medium-high heat. Once butter is melted add cream. Bring to a boil. Boil 3 minutes, stirring constantly. Turn off heat and stir in pecans and vanilla. A warning about this praline sauce. It's addictive! I mean, you could put this on a boot heel and it would be good. I serve it on my cheesecake, my ice cream, my well, anything sweet. It's just darn good.

Devotion

Let it rise!

I love making homemade bread. The whole kneading thing and getting flour from my eyebrows to my ankles is fun. Many a weekend I'm up to my hairline in flour and yeast. And, yes, I'm talking about the old-fashioned kneading-the-dough-with-your-own-two-hands kind of bread. (Confession, I do now own a KitchenAid mixer with a dough hook that would make a pirate jealous.) But sometimes I still do it all by hand. There's just something about the process.

I found a recipe that reminded me of my grandmother's divine dinner rolls. The instructions are quite specific. You dissolve the yeast in warm water, not hot. You add flour one cup at a time, not all at once. You use a wooden spoon not metal. After kneading for about ten minutes, you let the dough rise to double its size. Then you give it a good ole' punch in the face, and let it rise again. It's practically an all-day process. I often wonder which of my great, great, great grandmothers figured out this exact formula? Because when followed precisely, the payoff is stupendous! The bread is melt in your mouth delicious. When it's not followed to the 't' you've puttered all day in the kitchen to make hockey pucks.

Remember, the rising takes time. It cannot be rushed, and if you try to hurry it, the bread loses the very softness and strength it was meant to have. Our spiritual growth is no different. We want instant maturity, instant clarity, instant breakthrough. But God often works in the slow swell of hidden places, where no one sees the rising but Him.

There are seasons when God is stretching us, pressing us, folding us again and again, not because He is harsh, but because He is forming something inside us that can hold greater purpose. The kneading is not punishment. It is preparation. The "punching down" moments feel like we are losing progress or being flattened by life, but are often the very moments God is making room for a greater rise.

It is easy to praise God when the dough is rising, but the real shaping happens when we stay faithful while He works the air back out of us. God does not just want us to look like bread. He wants us to become nourishment to others, the kind of life that feeds and blesses those who are hungry for hope.

Sometimes the greatest work God does is in silence, in waiting, in the unseen hours where nothing looks finished yet. But He has not forgotten the recipe. He is intentional with every pause and every touch, every fold and every rise. If we stay in His hands long enough, we will see the beauty of His process, and we will taste the goodness of what He was making all along.

It reminds me that God has a process for us. There's no shortcut to becoming the man or woman of God we're supposed to be. Sometimes God "kneads" us and we need Him. Other times, we feel like we get a good ole' punch in the face. That's not the fun part to say the yeast, I mean least, but when we follow God's will and stick to His recipe of obedience, faithfulness and a big dose of prayer, the payoff is divine! Pass the butter, please!

SCRIPTURE (NIV):
"Being confident of this, that He who began a good work in you will carry it on to completion until the day of Christ Jesus."
— Philippians 1:6

PRAYER:
Lord, even when I cannot see the progress, remind me that You are still shaping me. Help me surrender to Your timing, Your process, and Your hands. Give me patience while I rise, courage when I feel pressed down, and faith that You will finish what You started in me. Make my life something that brings nourishment, comfort, and blessing to others. Amen.

The Softer Side of Cajun Cooking

Baking and desserts are my jam. But a girl can't live on bread pudding alone. Well, I probably could, but I'd be the size of a small school bus! I can exercise only so much. As the saying goes, you can't exercise away a bad diet. But I sure do try!

So, being a Louisiana girl, you would think I'd lean heavy on the hotness/spice scale, i.e. cayenne pepper when I'm cooking. But me and cayenne don't get along. Now I do keep some Panola Pepper (born right there in Lake Providence, Louisiana!) sauce in the pantry to take the heat up a notch when someone is expecting that pure Cajun taste. But I choose not to cook with cayenne. So if you're like me and have a sensitive palette but still want flavor, look no further. You're about to enter the zone for "the softer side of Cajun cooking"!

Tammi's tips for the softer side of Cajun cooking:

- Skip cayenne and go for chili powder instead.

- Use red or orange bell peppers instead of green. They're sweeter and less spicy

- Go heavy on black pepper. It intensifies the warmth of the dish without ramping up the spice level

- When using jalapeños always cut out the seeds and discard. And use gloves when handling hot peppers!

Crawfish Étouffée

½ stick of unsalted butter (¼ cup)
¼ cup all-purpose flour
1 small white onion, chopped (1 cup)
½ cup red or orange bell pepper, chopped
¼ cup celery hearts, chopped
2 tsp minced garlic
2 cups chicken stock/broth (can substitute seafood stock)
½ tsp kosher salt (go light on the salt if you're using Tony Chachere's seasoning)
black pepper, to taste
½ tsp Cajun blend seasoning (I normally use Tony Chachere's)
1 lb Louisiana Crawfish tails
1 Tbsp fresh parsley, chopped (plus extra for garnish)
¼ cup green onion, sliced (plus extra for garnish)

Start with what we in Louisiana call the Cajun trinity. Onion, bell pepper and celery. Chop them fine. Then chop your parsley and green onions; and garlic.

The roux can be the tricky part. (You can now buy pre-made roux in most grocery stores. But where's the fun in that?!) Start by melting butter in a large skillet over medium heat. Stir in the flour; and stir constantly until caramel colored. Usually takes 4 to 5 minutes.

To that, add the onion, bell pepper and celery; cook until soft. Next, add the garlic and cook until your kitchen smells divine.

Add the stock. Followed by salt, pepper and Cajun seasoning.

Bring it to a boil; reduce heat to a medium-low simmer, cover and simmer for 15 minutes, stirring occasionally.

Last, add the crawfish tails, cook and stir until crawfish is heated through; stir in parsley and green onion, reserving a bit for garnish.

Serve over rice, or I like to serve it over grits.

Blackened Catfish with Shellfish White Wine Sauce

Catfish:

1 tsp salt

1 tsp ground black pepper

1 tsp ground chili powder
   (cayenne if you like it hot)

1 tsp garlic powder

1 tsp onion powder

1 tsp paprika

1 tsp dried parsley

½ tsp dried oregano

½ tsp dried thyme

4 (4-oz) catfish fillets, skinned

¾ cup unsalted butter

Sauce:

2 shallots, finely chopped

1¼ cups white wine, dry
   (chardonnay is especially good)

1 tsp lemon juice

1 tsp white wine vinegar

⅛ tsp salt

1 pinch pepper

1 pinch white sugar

1 cup heavy cream

1 tbsp of Worcestershire sauce

½ a stick unsalted butter cut into ⅓" cubes

1 cup of fresh crab meat

12 medium-size Louisiana Gulf Shrimp

Catfish:

First, pat the catfish filets with a paper towel. You want them dry. Mix together all your seasonings in a shallow bowl until combined. Press catfish fillets into the spice mixture to thoroughly coat on both sides. Use a large cast iron skillet and place it over high heat. Put butter in the skillet and let it melt. When butter in the skillet is really hot, lay catfish fillets into the skillet. Cook until the spices are burned onto the fillets and the catfish is opaque and flaky inside, about 3 minutes per side. To serve, pour remaining ½ cup butter over the catfish.

Sauce:

Start by putting the chopped shallots, white wine, lemon juice, vinegar, salt, pepper, sugar to the pan. Bring to simmer and reduce by half.

Add cream, simmer for 2 minutes.

Turn heat to low and add cold butter one cube at a time while mixing with wooden spoon. Once all the butter is incorporated, the sauce should be thickened.

Next sauté or blacken the shrimp in the same pan that you used to blacken the catfish. Using the butter and spices. Do not overcook the shrimp. Just before serving, add the shrimp to the white wine sauce. Using more white wine to deglaze the pan. Add the Worcestershire sauce.

Place fish on the plate. Spoon some sauce over the fish. Enjoy!

Crab Cakes with Remoulade Sauce

Cakes:
1 small yellow onion
2 Tbsp butter
1 large egg
¼ cup mayonnaise
2 Tbsp chopped fresh parsley
1½ tsp seafood seasoning, such as Old Bay
1 tsp Dijon mustard
1 lemon, zested
1 pound lump crabmeat
½ cup panko breadcrumbs
2 Tbsp salted butter, melted
   (plus more for greasing the baking sheet)

Sauce:
1 cup mayonnaise
1 Tbsp capers, drained and chopped
½ tsp garlic salt
¼ tsp freshly ground black pepper
Juice of 1 lemon

Cakes:

Start by chopping and then sautéing the onion until onion is tender. Then combine the egg, mayonnaise, parsley, seafood seasoning, Dijon mustard and lemon zest all together. Add the cooked onion, crabmeat and breadcrumbs. Form crab cakes by pressing them into shape with a ⅓-cup measuring cup. Place on a buttered baking sheet. (I also cook them in the skillet as well but for this dish we'll bake them)

Turn on the broiler. You can brush the tops of the crab cakes with the melted butter. Do not put the pan close to the broiler as you would toast. Keep this about 8 inches away from the broiler. Broil until golden on top, 4 to 5 minutes. Serve immediately with the remoulade sauce.

Sauce:

Put the mayonnaise, capers, garlic salt, pepper and lemon juice to a bowl and whisk. (Sometimes I add Worcestershire sauce to mine because I like it!)

To fry the crab cakes: add the butter to the skillet over medium heat. Sear until golden, 3 to 4 minutes per side.

Roasted Corn Grits

2 ears fresh corn on the cob
   (or one can of whole kernel corn)
1 cup onion, chopped
2 garlic, cloves minced
4 Tbsp butter (¼ cup)
1 cup heavy whipping cream
1 cup yellow corn grits (not instant)
Chicken stock
   (in place of water for cooking grits
   according to package directions)
Salt and pepper

I like to use fresh corn when I have the time, but I've also made this using canned whole kernel corn. I roast or slightly char the kernels in a cast iron skillet. Be careful not to burn them.

If using fresh off the cob, remove husk and roast on the grill until slightly blackened. Using a knife carefully shave the corn from the cob. Then lightly chop the corn.

In a large skillet, melt the butter. Add onions and cook until tender; add garlic and cook until both are softened.

Take the chicken stock and pour it in a tall heavy bottom saucepan. Cook the grits according to the package directions.

When almost done, add the corn kernels, sauteed onions and garlic, and cream. Lower the heat and simmer, stirring constantly. Do this for about 5 minutes or longer until thickened. Season with salt and pepper. You can garnish with thinly sliced green onions.

Tammi's tip for best roasted corn on the cob:

Soak the corn in its husk in cold water for 30 minutes. Then place it on a hot grill, in its husk, for about 20 minutes. The corn can also be roasted in the oven for about 30 minutes. Once roasted, remove from husk and remove all silk.

Bourbon and Brown Sugar Baked Salmon

2-4 salmon filets, skinless and clean
2 Tbsp chives, chopped
1 cup bourbon
¼ cup pineapple juice
2 Tbsp soy sauce
2 Tbsp brown sugar
A dash of salt
A dash of ground black pepper
A pinch of garlic powder
1 Tbsp olive oil

You'll want to marinate the salmon filets for a few hours before cooking. I've even marinated them overnight but found that's too much. The Bourbon doesn't "cook off" if you marinate them too long.

Line up your filets in an oblong or square baking dish (big enough for filets to lay side by side. In a separate bowl or measuring cup, combine the pineapple juice, brown sugar, bourbon, and soy sauce until sugar dissolves.

Add the salt, pepper and garlic powder. Mix well.

Pour the marinade over the fish. Flip them a couple of times to make sure they're completely covered.

Put them in the refrigerator and let the fish marinate for at least half an hour up to two hours.

Take fish out of the fridge while you pre-heat your oven to 375°F. (You want the filets to be room temp before baking)

Line a baking sheet with foil and place the filets on the sheet.

Pour any excess marinade on the filets. Bake 12 to 15 minutes.

Roasted Brussels Sprouts

1 lb Brussels sprouts, cleaned and trimmed
3 cloves garlic, peeled and sliced
¼ cup Parmesan Cheese, freshly grated
salt and black pepper to taste
3 Tbsp olive oil
¼ cup molasses
1 tsp nutmeg
1 Tbsp thyme
2 Tbsp Balsamic vinegar

Sauce: (optional)
4 cups raspberries
1 Tbsp cane sugar
½ cup soy sauce
½ cup honey
¼ cup light brown sugar
1 tsp garlic powder
1 tsp apple cider vinegar
¼ tsp salt

Preheat your oven to 400°F. While it's preheating, cut off the hard stems of the sprouts. Then, cut each sprout in half. Keep any leaves that fall off and all to mixing bowl. (It's easier to get good coverage on each sprout by putting them in a mixing bowl and then transferring to baking sheet.)

Add the garlic, salt, and pepper, thyme, nutmeg, molasses, balsamic vinegar and olive oil. Toss around in the bowl until each bulb is coated.

Roast in the oven uncovered for 20 to 25 minutes until crisp, brown and caramelized on the outside and tender on the inside. Remove from oven and sprinkle with Parmesan cheese.

Optional sauce: I sometimes add a raspberry chipotle sauce to Brussels sprouts right when they come out of the oven. But they're great without it! But in case you want to take this one step further. Here you go!

You'll start by roasting your raspberries. So, preheat the oven to 375°F. I use parchment paper to line the baking sheet because it's easier for cleanup. Then, I spray the paper with cooking spray. Spread out the raspberries on the sheet so they're not touching. You want to roast them, not steam them. Sprinkle on the sugar. Roast for 15 minutes.

Remove from the oven and let them cool for 10 to15 minutes. Put the roasted raspberries and the remaining ingredients in a food processor. I have also used a handheld blender to do this. Blend until pureed!

Turkey and Sausage Gumbo

1 Tbsp vegetable oil

1 lb andouille sausage, chopped
  (use smoked if you don't like the spice of
  andouille)

4 Tbsp unsalted butter

1 cup chopped onion

½ cup chopped celery

½ cup chopped green (or red) bell pepper

3 cloves garlic, minced

½ cup all-purpose flour

1 tsp salt

1 tsp smoked paprika

½ tsp ground black pepper

1 qt leftover turkey pan juices
   (or turkey stock or chicken stock)

2 cups leftover chopped or shredded cooked turkey

2 bay leaves

1 Tbsp fresh thyme leaves

1 Tbsp fresh lemon juice

1 lb fresh or frozen okra

¼ tsp Worcestershire sauce

Hot cooked rice

In a tall, heavy bottom pot, heat vegetable oil over medium-high heat. Add the chopped sausage, and cook for 8 to 10 minutes or until browned. Take out the sausage, and set aside, but leave the drippings in pot.

Add the butter to the drippings over medium-high heat. Stir in onion and next put in celery, bell pepper and garlic. Cook until tender, about 6 to 8 minutes. Sprinkle in flour, salt, pepper and paprika; cook, stirring constantly, for 1 minute.

Next, pour and whisk in turkey juices or stock until well combined. Add turkey, thyme, lemon juice, Worcestershire, and cooked sausage; bring to a boil. Reduce heat, cover, and simmer, stirring occasionally. Add the okra last, about ten minutes before you're ready to serve. You'll cook for another for 10 to 12 minutes or until slightly thickened. Serve over rice.

Crawfish (or Shrimp) Creole

**1 package Crawfish tails
  (or shrimp)**
¼ cup olive or canola oil
8 oz smoked sausage
1 medium onion chopped
¼ cup celery, diced
**1 small bell pepper, chopped
  (use red or orange)**
1-2 tsp fresh thyme
2 tsp minced garlic
1 bay leaf
2 tsp creole seasoning or more
7-14 oz stewed tomatoes
2 cups or more chicken broth
1 tsp Worcestershire sauce
1-2 green onions, chopped
2 Tbsp parsley, chopped

Dust the shrimp with your Creole/Cajun spices of your choice. In a large skillet, put in 1 tablespoon of oil over medium heat. (You do not need to do this if using crawfish tails. We'll add and season them later)

Sauté shrimp for about 1to 2 minutes. Just until barely pink. Next, add your sausage sauté until browned on both sides and remove from pan.

In the same pan, add remaining oil. Then place your onions, celery, bell pepper, thyme and garlic. Stir for about a 2 to 3 minutes. Add the bay leaf and more Cajun spices. I usually use Tony Chachere's. Next add stewed tomatoes, chicken broth, and Worcestershire sauce.

Bring to a boil, simmer for 10 to 15 minutes.

Finally, toss in shrimp, sausage and green onions. (If you use crawfish tails put them in now and add a little more salt and pepper to the tails) Cook for about 2 to 3 more minutes. Garnish with parsley. Serve over white rice or grits.

Shrimp and Grits

Grits:
2 cups heavy cream
4 Tbsp salted butter (½ stick)
½ tsp salt
6 cups of chicken stock
2 cups dry grits (not instant)

Shrimp:
8 oz bacon, chopped
2 large onions, sliced thin julienne-style
⅓ cup garlic, minced
2 red bell pepper, sliced thin
2 green bell pepper, sliced thin julienne-style
2 sticks salted butter
1 Tbsp Cajun seasoning plus more for seasoning
1 tsp cayenne pepper (optional)
2 Tbsp Vegetable oil
2 lb large gulf shrimp, peeled and deveined
Salt to taste

I use chicken stock instead of water to make my grits. It's just better. So, in a large pot, combine the cream, butter, salt and 6 cups of chicken stock. Bring to a boil over moderate heat.

Stir in the grits. Lower the heat and simmer until creamy, about 10 minutes. Keep an eye on it because it can bubble up and overflow the pot.

Let's prepare the shrimp. In a large skillet, cook the bacon over moderate heat until crisp. Transfer the bacon to a paper towel-lined plate. Leave the bacon drippings in the skillet.

Add the onion and garlic. Cook until the onion is translucent, about 5 minutes. Next, add bell peppers and one stick of butter and simmer another 10 minutes.

Add Cajun seasoning and salt to taste. Cook 2 more minutes.

Time now for the remaining stick of butter, turn off the heat. Stir the sauce until the butter is melted.

In a separate skillet, we'll prepare the shrimp with Cajun seasoning. Add the oil to the skillet and heat the oil until shimmering. Add shrimp and sauté until lightly pink, about 2 minutes.

Serve by placing ½ cup of grits into a shallow bowl. Top with a large scoop of shrimp sauce and 6 large shrimp. Garnish with bacon.

Corn and Crab Bisque

3 Tbsp butter
3 Tbsp all-purpose flour
1 Tbsp vegetable oil
1 large onion, chopped
1 Tbsp garlic, minced
1 large celery stalk, minced
Cajun seasoning to taste
1 cup chicken broth
1 ½ cups frozen corn kernels
1 bay leaf
2 cups milk
2 cups heavy cream
1 tsp crab boil seasoning
1 lb fresh lump crabmeat
¼ cup green onions, chopped
½ tsp Worcestershire sauce
Salt and pepper to taste

Start by melting the butter in a small pot over medium heat. Now we'll make a roux. Gradually whisk in the flour. You'll need to cook the flour 5 to 7 minutes, whisking constantly, until a golden roux forms.

Put your oil in a large pot or Dutch oven over medium heat. Add the onion, garlic, and celery and cook 1 minute.

Next, put in the Cajun seasoning. Followed by the broth, corn, and bay leaf. Bring to a simmer.

Next, pour in the milk, cream, and crab boil. When you start to see it bubble, reduce heat to low and simmer 7 minutes. Stir in the roux, 1 tablespoon at a time.

Cook on low heat, whisking until mixture thickens.

Final step is stirring in crabmeat, green onions, and Worcestershire sauce. Simmer 6 to 8 minutes more. Give it the taste test and see if it needs more salt or pepper.

Tammi tip: Go light on the crab boil. It can be very spicy. So if you have kids who'll be eating this dish or you're like me, and have a sensitive palette, I add very little or omit it altogether.

Lettuce Pray
I'll have the Cheeseburger

Waiter asks: "Will you have the cheeseburger or spinach salad?"

Really, you have to ask?"

When I get to Heaven, one of the things I want to ask God is why He made cheeseburgers and pizza taste so much better than spinach and celery? I will also ask Him why He gave me the metabolism of a snail. I've always had to be careful with calories, but as the calendar keeps flipping pages, it gets increasingly difficult to keep the poundage off. I have friends who can eat anything they want, exercise never, and they never have to buy pants with an elastic waistband! It's not fair!

But I must remember that God didn't promise us fair; He promised us forever.

He didn't promise us happiness; He promised us peace.

God didn't promise us we'd be rich; He promised us we'd be richly blessed.

I still don't think it's fair that I'm not able to eat all the cheeseburgers, mac and cheese, and cheesecake that I want. But I also remember that God says we should eat to live, not live to eat.

More spinach salad, please!

Devotion

The older we get, the more we realize that discipline is rarely about desire, it is about wisdom. Our taste buds crave comfort, but our bodies thrive on what nourishes us. Spiritually, it works the very same way. The easy thing, the feel-good thing, the thing that satisfies us at the moment, is almost never the thing that sustains us long-term.

We live in a world filled with "cheeseburger choices" for the soul. All the quick fixes, comfort distractions, emotional fillers, and temporary highs that feel good going down, often leave us sluggish, empty, or weighed down on the inside. Meanwhile, the things that help us grow are often quieter, slower, and less glamorous: prayer, stillness, obedience, humility, forgiveness, and choosing what is right when no one is clapping for us.

Just like the body feels the consequences of what we consume, our spirit feels the consequences of what we feed it. A steady diet of convenience faith cannot produce deep strength. But when we choose what nourishes us over what merely entertains us, we find a kind of peace and stability that no earthly comfort can imitate.

We may not always crave the "spinach salad" version of spiritual growth, but over time, our appetite changes. The more we walk with God, the more we begin to desire what aligns with Him. True maturity is when we stop asking, "What do I want right now?" and begin asking, "What will bring life to me tomorrow?"

God is not withholding pleasure from us. He is protecting purpose in us. His ways shape us so that we are healthy on the inside, not just momentarily happy on the outside.

SCRIPTURE (NIV):
"No discipline seems pleasant at the time, but painful. Later on, however, it produces a harvest of righteousness and peace for those who have been trained by it."
— Hebrews 12:11

PRAYER:
Lord, help me choose what nourishes me, not just what comforts me. Strengthen my spirit to walk in wisdom and self-control. Teach me to desire the things that lead to life, peace, and closeness with You. Grow in me a hunger for what makes me spiritually whole. Amen.

Now let's get to making some cookies.

I've come up with my own sugar cookie recipe that is unlike any other. And I've been told that my cookies are da' best!

Sugar Cookies

1½ cups butter, softened
½ cup shortening
1 cup granulated sugar
1 large egg
1 tsp orange zest
1 Tbsp vanilla extract
¼ cup cream cheese, softened
¼ cup of sour cream
½ tsp baking powder
3 cups all-purpose flour
pinch of salt
½ tsp of cinnamon
½ tsp of cardamom

Put the butter and shortening in your stand mixer. Combine. Then slowly add the cup of sugar.

Cream the butter and sugar.

Zest the orange and add to the mixer. Then add your egg and vanilla. Next, add the cream cheese and sour cream.

In a separate bowl, add the flour, baking powder, pinch of salt, cinnamon and cardamom. Add the flour mixture to your mixing bowl. Mix it only until the flour is incorporated into the dough.

Divide the dough into two sections and wrap in plastic wrap. Place this in the refrigerator and chill for at least four hours.

Take out the dough and let it rest for about 30 minutes. Roll out the dough and cut out the desired shapes with your cookie cutters. Put the tray of cookies back in the fridge while preheating your oven to 375°F (chilling the dough again helps the cookies retain their shape).

Bake the cookies for about 8 to 10 minutes depending on the size of the cookie. Take out of the oven just when the edges start to turn golden brown. Put them on a cooling rack. Let them cool completely before decorating.

Tips for Decorating Sugar Cookies without Losing Your Mind

There's something magical about a tray of decorated sugar cookies. The glossy icing, the tiny details, the sprinkle sparkle, it's edible art! But if you've ever found yourself elbow-deep in royal icing wondering how the bakers on Pinterest make it look so easy, you're not alone. The secret? Patience, practice, and a whole lot of powdered sugar.

A good cookie starts before the icing even comes out. My sugar cookie recipe on the previous page is the best place to start.

Royal Icing is Your Friend: Now let's talk about Royal Icing. I'd never heard of royal icing before I started my cookie decorating journey. This is the type of icing that will dry and harden on the cookie so you can decorate it. But yet it still tastes good. But let me tell you, royal icing consistency is a trick you have to master. And if your consistency is off when you start decorating, then you're headed for disaster. Recipe on page 54.

> *Tip: Add color a little at a time as gel food coloring is very vibrant without watering down your icing. Keep in mind, too, that colors darken when they dry, so think of going a shade or two lighter than you need.*

Be Patient: The cookies need to dry for several hours, ideally overnight, before you add layers or details. This is your cue to step away, make tea, and admire your first batch from afar. Decorating cookies is a marathon, not a sprint. If you try to rush, you'll end up with colors bleeding into each other or icing that collapses like a bad soufflé.

Tip: If patience isn't your strong suit, use a fan or food dehydrator on low to speed up drying time safely.

Design Like You're Playing: Think of each cookie as a mini canvas, not a test. Sketch ideas on paper or use cookie cutters as stencils to plan. Keep it simple: dots, lines, and swirls can look elegant. You don't have to pipe the Mona Lisa onto a mitten.

Tip: Try a few "practice cookies" to warm up your piping hand, those first few wobbly lines are totally normal.

Tools Make a Difference: Piping bags, scribe tools, and toothpicks are your best friends. A toothpick can smooth edges, pop bubbles, and even draw designs in wet icing. Keep a damp paper towel handy to wipe tips between colors or when switching bags.

Tip: If piping bags feel intimidating, start with squeeze bottles, they're easier to control and less likely to splatter.

Layer, Add Texture, and Have Fun: Once the base is dry, add new colors or textures: polka dots, stripes, or even edible glitter. Want that trendy "snowy sweater" look? Use a thick consistency icing and a small star tip to pipe cozy patterns.

Tip: For quick dimension, let each color dry for 15–20 minutes before adding the next, it keeps them crisp and raised instead of blending together.

Give Yourself Grace and a Cookie: Perfection is overrated. The joy of cookie decorating is in the process, not just the picture. Your slightly crooked Christmas tree or lopsided heart will still taste amazing, and it might even make someone smile more than a flawless one.

Tip: Snap a photo of your cookies anyway. You'll be amazed at how much you improve each time! Decorating sugar cookies isn't about being perfect, it's about spreading a little sweetness. So, turn on your favorite playlist, grab a piping bag, and remember: even if your icing runs wild, that's just more reason to taste test.

How I Became the Crazy Cookie Lady

This section is dedicated to my crazy cookie-decorating obsession. Those who grew up with me know that I have little-to-no artistic talent. I can barely draw a stick man! But yet, I can decorate sugar cookies with royal icing that some say look like works of art. I can't explain it. I still can't draw a stick man if you give me pen and paper but give me a piping bag and some royal icing and the artwork flows! Let me tell you how it all started. Cause that's a crazy story.

I got a call from my former general manager at WKRN, the ABC affiliate in Nashville, Mike Sechrist. He had become the GM at WOWK in Charleston, WV. I was working for RFD-TV, the agriculture network, based out of Nashville. Mike said Tammi, I think you'd be perfect as our main anchor at WOWK. And I said, where? He said Charleston, the other Charleston.

I just knew it would be too cold and too far from home [Louisiana]. But Mike not only offered me the prime-time anchor chair, but he also said I could have my own weekly cooking segment. Well, that sealed the deal! I had been dreaming of having my own cooking show. So I told RFD I had been offered a job and planned to turn in my notice. (I was secretly hoping RFD would ask me to stay and offer me a raise. Or at least offer me a Starbucks card or a Honey Baked Ham! But they offered to show me the door and wished me well.) So off to Charleston I went. And Mike kept his word. He let me start my weekly cooking show. I called it the WOWKitchen (get it? For WOWK?)

Boy, that was more work than I ever thought it would be. First, the planning of the dishes, the grocery shopping, the cooking the dish BEFORE the shoot (because you had to have a finished dish ready to show to the camera at the end of that 4 minute segment—cause nothing cooks in 4 minutes! Lol) Then, prepping the kitchen the day of the shoot. If you notice on cooking shows, the kitchens are pristine. Never a dish out of place. The ingredients are magically already measured and all utensils are within arm's reach. I don't know about you, but in my kitchen, that's not how things go down on a daily basis. So prep work is a huge undertaking. And let's not talk about the cleanup process!

After only a few weeks into my new "dream" job of having my own cooking segment, I come to the realization that my repertoire of recipes, both sweet and savory, is probably in the neighborhood of about 2 dozen. That's 24 recipes that I have committed to memory and can pull off without having to consult a cookbook or Google. Since WOWK found a sponsor for this weekly segment, I was now obligated for a year. I would need to make 52 dishes in front of the camera without cheating and looking at a recipe! So I decided I needed to invite local chefs to be part of my segment. One of those guests was Linda Childers of Milton, WV. She was an artist. Like a true "art you hang on the wall' artist. But she also decorated sugar cookies, using cookies as her canvas. Her cookies deserved to be framed. After shooting our segment that day, I said, I could never do anything like that because I can't draw a tic-tac-toe diagram! She assured me that I could do it. If I just knew a few of the basic techniques and got my icing consistency correct. Not long after her visit to WOWK, it was another stupid, cold, wintery day in West Virginia. (And remember, I'm an outdoors girl, but it has to be 55 degrees or above or I won't venture out!). So I called Linda and asked if she'd show me some of her cookie decorating techniques. She graciously agreed. I had very low expectations. Not of her. But of me! She also pointed me in the direction of some great cookie decorators on YouTube. So, nearly every weekend for the remainder of that winter, I practiced cookie decorating with royal icing. I knew I could make a knock your socks off "tasting" sugar cookie. Now I wanted them to be as beautiful as they were delicious. And so the obsession was born. I believe that was 2015. Now I'm the crazy cookie lady!

Devotion

You can underestimate yourself, but never underestimate God! It's not about how much talent you have but how much you allow yourself to be teachable and used by Him. You may have talents hidden that just need a little nudge to come out and play on a cold winter's day, like I did with Linda!

Here's what I learned from that experience. You can underestimate yourself, but never underestimate God! You may have talents hidden that just need a little nudge to come out and play on a cold winter's day, like I did with Linda!

Sometimes God places gifts inside of us that do not surface until we are willing to step into something unfamiliar or uncomfortable. We say, "I can't," but God whispers, "You haven't tried yet." We measure ourselves by what we already know how to do, while God sees what we could do if we yielded our hands to Him. Hidden gifts only stay hidden when fear or self-doubt convinces us not to try.

God is not looking for perfection; He is looking for willingness. The moment we put our abilities, however small they feel, into His hands, He multiplies them. That is why some of the greatest works in our lives are born not from confidence, but from obedience. What begins as a timid step of curiosity can become a calling, a blessing, or a ministry we never saw coming.

There is beauty in knowing that God is still unveiling us. There is more inside of you than you think. More creativity, more grace, more strength, and more purpose. Sometimes all it takes is saying yes to the nudge, the invitation, or even the boredom of a winter day where He says, "Let Me show you what I've tucked inside of you."

When God breathes on a gift, it becomes more than a hobby… it becomes a testimony.

SCRIPTURE (NIV):
"Now to him who is able to do immeasurably more than all we ask or imagine, according to his power that is at work within us."
— Ephesians 3:20

PRAYER:
Lord, thank You for the gifts You've placed inside me — even the ones I have not discovered yet. Help me to stay teachable, courageous, and willing so that You can draw out what You planted long ago. Use my hands for Your glory, and remind me that with You nothing is wasted, and nothing is impossible. Amen.

Royal Icing

**4 Tbsp meringue powder
(or two egg whites)**
**4 cups powdered sugar
(about 1 lb)**
**5 Tbsp water
(+ more depending on the
consistency of the icing you
need)**
1 tsp clear vanilla extract
½ tsp light corn syrup
½ tsp of cream of tartar

Start with a very clean bowl on your stand mixer. Whisk together the meringue powder and powdered sugar, and cream of tartar. Next, add the corn syrup, the water and vanilla extract. Definitely use the paddle attachment for this (not the whisk) otherwise you'll incorporate too many air bubbles. Run the mixer for a good five minutes. This increases the intensity of the white. From here, you need to decide what consistency you need.

Here are the most common consistencies you need for decorating your cookies with Royal Icing:
- Stiff consistency (good for brush embroidery and 3D details)
- 15-second or 3D consistency (good for 3D details)
- Piping consistency (good for outlining and detailing)
- Flooding consistency

Flooding consistency royal icing is a thinner, runnier icing that "floods" the large area of the cookies. It's the fastest way to completely cover a cookie in icing. Make it too runny and you'll be left with a mess as it flows over your piping. Make it too stiff and it won't spread or set smoothly. So consistency is key!

I usually make a flood and piping consistency of each color I need. This is also where you color your icing. I always use gel food coloring instead of water-based. It gives a bolder color, plus the water-based food coloring will impact your consistency.

The way I learned my decorating techniques, besides what I picked up from Linda on that snowy afternoon, was through YouTube tutorials. If you just Google cookie decorating, you'll get thousands. But here are some of my go-to decorators on YouTube: Julia Usher, SweetAmbs, My Little Bakery, and Haniela's.

Gingerbread Cutout Cookies

¾ cup butter, softened
1 cup packed brown sugar
1 large egg, room temperature
¾ cup molasses
4 cups all-purpose flour
2 tsp ground ginger
½ tsp baking soda
1 ½ tsp ground cinnamon
¾ tsp ground cloves
¼ tsp salt

Start by creaming together the butter and brown sugar in the bowl of your stand mixer. You want this to turn into something light and fluffy. Next, add egg and molasses.

In a separate bowl, sift the flour, ginger, baking soda, cinnamon, cloves and salt. Slowly add to creamed mixture. I often spoon in the flour mixture a cup at a time. Mix well.

Separate the dough into two pieces and wrap in plastic wrap. Refrigerate for about 4 hours or overnight.

Roll the dough onto a floured surface. I usually try to roll out to ⅛" thickness. Cut out the desired shapes with cookie cutters.

Place baking sheets covered with parchment or Silpat.

Bake for 8 to 10 minutes. Remove from oven and place on cooling racks.

Tammi's tips for the best cutout cookies:

- Don't skimp on ingredients. Don't buy off-brands. I buy the highest quality flour and use unbleached all-purpose.

- If you use another recipe for your cutout cookies, it's a good idea never to use more than ½ tsp of baking powder. Keeping the leavening agent to a minimum helps the cookie keep its shape. But don't skip it altogether. That impacts the texture of the cookie.

- Chilling the dough and chilling it again just before baking is also key in helping the cookie keep its shape and not spread.

- I like a real, tender, soft and chewy cookie. So, I tend to underbake my cookies just a tad. This is also helpful because sometimes I use a dehydrator when getting my royal icing to dry faster, and I don't want the cookie to dry out.

- When using cookie cutters with lots of corners and curves, it's best to dip the cutter in some flour or powdered sugar before cutting the dough.

- I prefer to use powdered sugar to "flour" my counter when rolling out the dough. This way, I don't continue adding flour to the dough. This can dry out your cookie.

Chocolate Cutout Cookies

1 cup unsalted butter, cubed, softened
¼ cup vegetable shortening
1½ cup granulated sugar
3½ cup all-purpose flour
⅔ cup unsweetened cocoa powder
½ tsp baking powder
½ tsp salt
2 eggs, room temperature
1 tsp vanilla extract
2 tsp espresso powder
** (or instant coffee granules)**

You'll want to marinate the salmon filets for a few hours before cooking. I've even marinated them Start by sifting together the flour, cocoa powder, baking powder, and salt.

Then, in the bowl of your stand mixer, cream together butter, shortening, and sugar. This should transform to a light-colored mixture.

In a measuring cup or bowl, stir together eggs, vanilla, and espresso powder. Add to the butter and sugar mixture until combined.

Add the flour mixture. I add it one cup at a time. Beat on medium speed.

Continue mixing until all dry ingredients are added, and the dough begins to pull away from the side of the mixing bowl

Divide the dough into two disks and wrap in plastic wrap. Chill for at least 4 hours.

When ready to bake, roll out cookie dough to about 1/4 inch thickness on a floured or cocoa surface. Cut into desired shapes with cookie cutters. Place on a baking sheet covered with parchment or a Silpat.

Put the tray back in the refrigerator.

Preheat the oven to 375°F. Bake for 7 to 9 minutes. Let cool on the baking sheet for 5 minutes, then transfer to a wire rack to cool completely.

Recipes I Ate as a Kid

If you didn't grow up in the country or in my generation (or earlier), you will not appreciate this next chapter. I've mentioned before that my dad was a hunter. There was always a gun in the truck or the house. He mainly hunted deer, but he was known to shoot a duck, a squirrel, an alligator or a snake if it found its unfortunate way into our yard. But seldom did a critter's ultimate sacrifice go to waste. My daddy could make a stew out of anything. So yes, we ate squirrel. And to this day, I love a good duck breast and will eat anything fried in duck fat! Daddy also cooked chitterlings, or as we say, chitlins'. If you don't know what they are, well, it's hog intestines! Yep. We ate them. But more importantly, Daddy cooked them. And Lord have mercy on my soul, they stank to high heaven. We had to leave the house when Daddy got that big ole pot boiling. He wasn't allowed to cook them inside. Mama put her foot down on that! He had to use the carport. You boil them for hours. And believe it or not, the Piggly Wiggly near my house at the writing of this cookbook, has chitlins! So, I decided I'd give them a whirl myself. (won't do that again!)

Other things I grew up on, that to this day, I love to eat. A tomato (fresh from the garden or farmer's market) and mayo sandwich, a potted meat sandwich, and fried bologna. Kids today would probably turn up their noses at those items, but I love them.

We weren't known for entertaining at our house. Oh, Mom had her friends who would drop by for coffee. I remember Ella Ruth Hopkins and Mrs. Horn (can't remember her first name but she was also our Avon lady!). Then there were Martha Wade and Sandra Smith—Mom's running buddies after Mom and Dad got divorced. They were always up to something fun, but I don't ever remember it being centered around food. If we had "appetizers," it consisted of a block of cream cheese covered in pepper jelly or just plain old cheese and crackers. Fancy we weren't.

Chitterlings

10 lb frozen chitterlings, thawed and cleaned
1 onion, roughly chopped
2 tsp salt
1 tsp minced garlic
1 Tbsp of black pepper

Devotion

Some people believe hospitality is about presentation, such as the perfect appetizer table, themed napkins, spotless counters, and recipes that look like a magazine cover. But real hospitality has never been about perfection. It has always been about presence. It is not the table that welcomes people, it is the heart.

When I think back on those simple visits of coffee at the kitchen table, laughter without a menu, friendships not fueled by presentation, I see something holy in it. There was no pressure to impress, only space to belong. Sometimes the most meaningful fellowship is a block of cream cheese and pepper jelly shared with people who actually know you and love you, anyway.

God never asked us to entertain. He asked us to make room in our hearts, our schedules, and our lives for others. Some of the warmest memories are born out of simplicity, not extravagance, because love does not need decoration to be real.

We live in a world that tells us to polish everything before we let people in, but Jesus often ministered at dusty tables, ordinary homes, and everyday moments. The Gospel does not require fancy, just available.

SCRIPTURE (NIV):
"Offer hospitality to one another without grumbling." — 1 Peter 4:9 (NIV)

PRAYER:
Lord, teach me to value connection over perfection. Help me open my heart and my home with freedom, not pressure. Remind me that love is enough, even when the table is simple and the offering is small. Let whoever enters my life feel welcomed, seen, and cared for, because You were welcomed here first. Amen.

You'll need a large pot for this. In Louisiana, we call it the crawfish pot because it's usually what we boil crawfish or shrimp in, but it doesn't have to be that big. A 6-quart pot is good. Put your cleaned chitterlings in the pot and cover with cold water.

Once it has come to a rolling boil, add onion and salt, garlic, and pepper.

Cook until chitterlings are clear to white in color and reach desired tenderness. It will take at least 3 to 4 hours.

Cleaning and Handling Raw Chitterlings:

Soak chitterlings in cold water throughout the cleaning stage. Each chitterling should be examined and run under cold water, and all foreign materials should be removed and discarded. Chitterlings should retain some fat, so be careful to leave some on. After each chitterling has been cleaned, soak in two cold water baths for a few minutes. The second water bath should be clearer. If not, soak in one more bath.

Pepper Jelly

1½ cup red bell pepper, finely chopped and seeded

1 cup yellow bell pepper, finely chopped and seeded

1¼ cup green bell pepper, finely chopped and seeded

¼ cup jalapeño pepper, finely chopped and seeded

1 cup apple cider vinegar

1.75 oz package powdered pectin

5 cups sugar

1 canning pot

6-8 oz canning jars with lids and bands

You will need to sterilize your jars and lids. Do this by putting them in boiling water for several minutes.

Take all of your finely chopped and seeded peppers and put them in a large pot and turn heat on high.

Pour in the apple cider vinegar and powder fruit pectin. Stir constantly. Bring to a rolling boil. Remove from heat.

Now, add the sugar and put it back on high heat. Return to a boil for one minute.

Remove from heat. Skim off any foam from top.

Scoop the jelly into sterile jars, filling to ¼ inch from top of jar. Cover with lids.

Next, place those jars into canner with hot water that is not boiling. Water should completely cover jar. Cook on high heat until it reaches a boil. Process for 5 minutes. Remove from heat.

She's too Big for her Britches

My mom used to have a saying: she's too big for her britches. Which means someone is arrogant or disrespectful and conceited.

For me, it means a few too many cupcakes, and I'm literally too big for my britches!

But I understand what Mama meant.

It's easy for us to think more of ourselves than we should. It's human nature for us to say, look what I did. But it's hard for God to use a pious or prideful person. They're too busy telling people how great they think they are to do something great.

God likes to do extraordinary things through ordinary people. He's done it all through history. He's used stutterers, cheaters, crooks, and sheep herders to show out on his behalf.

It doesn't take a mastermind to make a miracle. It takes a man or a woman of God surrendering his or her selfish desires to the Savior's calling. It's being willing to give someone the shirt off your back or walking a few miles in someone else's boots and never getting too big for your britches.

Devotion

Humility is not thinking less of ourselves, it is thinking of ourselves less. Pride puts us at the center. Humility puts God back in His rightful place. When our hearts stay small before Him, His power can be seen more clearly through us. But when we get "too big for our britches," we start believing the spotlight belongs to us instead of the One who gave us the gift in the first place.

God delights in using the humble because humility leaves room for Him to move. When we believe we already have all the answers, we stop listening. When we believe we deserve the credit, we stop giving God the glory. But when we remember we are vessels, not the source, God can pour more through us.

The world teaches us to build a name. The Kingdom teaches us to lift up His name. The world applauds those who stand tallest. The Kingdom celebrates those who kneel first. God can do more with a surrendered heart than He can with a polished résumé. He is not looking for flawless people; He is looking for willing ones.

The greatest irony of walking with God is that the lower we bow, the higher He can lift us. Every miracle, every breakthrough, every open door becomes a testimony instead of a personal trophy. Because when the glory belongs to Him, the blessing stays clean, and the heart stays soft.

SCRIPTURE (NIV):
"Humble yourselves before the Lord, and He will lift you up."
— James 4:10 (NIV)

PRAYER:
Lord, keep my heart soft, my spirit teachable, and my pride in check. Remind me that anything good in me comes from You. Help me stay small in my own eyes so that You can be big in my life. Use me not because of my strength, but because of my surrender. Amen.

A Simple Place Setting

Many people feel unsure about how to set a table, but it's easier than it looks. Once you learn the basics of a simple place setting, you'll be able to do it effortlessly for family dinners, holidays, or any special occasion.

Many people feel unsure about how to set a table, but it's easier than it looks. Once you learn the basics of a simple place setting, you'll be able to do it effortlessly for family dinners, holidays, or any special occasion.

Here's how to set a simple place setting:

Start with the plate: Place the dinner plate in the center of the setting.

Add the napkin and fork: Lay the napkin to the left of the plate and place the fork on top of the napkin.

Place the knife and spoon: Set the knife to the right of the plate, with the blade facing inward toward the plate. Then place the spoon to the right of the knife.

Add the glass: Position the water glass just above the knife, slightly to the right.

That's it! Once you know this simple layout, you'll be able to set a neat, inviting table with confidence every time.

Tea Guide

CHAMOMILE
reduces stress & tension
supports digestion
boosts immunity
fights bacteria

CINNAMON
increases focus
calms upset stomach
improves digestive health
boosts immune system

LEMONGRASS
helps cholesterol
lowers blood pressure
relieves fluid retention
skin & hair health

DANDELION
helps weight loss
improves digestion
promotes strong bones
protects against anemia

EUCALYPTUS
helps boost energy
stimulates immune system
soothes stiffness & swelling
helps stress, mental fatigue

FENNEL
helps acid reflux
increases menstrual flow
heartburn treatments
natural diuretic

GREEN
controls free radicals
reduces cancer risk
helps prevent heart disease
assists with weight loss

VIOLET
helps ease severe headaches
anti-inflammatory
helps muscle inflammation,
& skin rashes

UVA URSI
known as 'Bearberry'
antibacterial
reduces water retention
boosts immune system

THYME
remedy for sore throats
helps gastrointestinal
discomfort & diarrhoea
reduces headache pain

SPEARMINT
helpful in treating colic & gas
helps improve digestion
anti-inflammatory
treats nausea & vomiting

YARROW
encourages menstruation by
stimulating uterus circulation
helps with symptoms
of mastitis

ROSEMARY
reduces headaches
promotes circulation
protects from oxidative stress
relieves cold symptoms

PEPPERMINT
anti-inflammatory
helps gastrointestinal issues
eases nausea
aids digestion

JASMINE
effective weight loss aid
increases metabolism
helps lower cholesterol
decreases artery inflammation

GINSENG
anti-carcinogenic components
helps fight obesity
eases stomach problems
helps constipation

GINGER
helps with symptoms of
irritable bowel syndrome
prevents heartburn
anti-inflammatory

FEVERFEW
helps reduce migraines,
treats nausea & vomiting
may help decrease the
duration of an illness

AMACHA
helps strengthen the
kidneys & urinary tract
caffeine-free
naturally sweet

CATNIP
helps induce a relaxed mind
reduces cramping
increases perspiration to
help treat colds

HIBISCUS
decreases anxiety
helps reduce blood pressure
calms the nervous system
promotes weight loss

JUNIPER BERRY
helps gastrointestinal health
good for skin health
antioxidant & antibacterial
good source of vitamin c

HAWTHORN
regulates blood pressure
heals skin ailments
provides an energy boost
helps blood circulation

HYSSOP
helps control blood sugar
aids in weight loss
digestive benefits
eases coughs & colds

LEMON BALM
calming effect
helps reduce insomnia
relieves indigestion/nausea
helps fight the herpes virus

OREGANO
anti-inflammatory
rich in antioxidants
helps reduce free radicals
anti-cancer properties

MARJORAM
promotes digestive health
reduces high blood pressure
helps manage diabetes by
improving insulin tolerance

ECHINACEA
helps ease bronchitis
strengthens immune system
helps manage anxiety
reduces inflammation

KAVA
aids in stress reduction
helps with anxiety
may reduce smoking cravings
helps with premature aging

PATCHOULI
helps with headaches & colds
treats nausea & vomiting
improves sexual desire
helps fight depression

Coffee Guide

AFFOGATO

ICE CREAM
- ESPRESSO

AMERICANO

WATER
- ESPRESSO

BREVE

MILK FOAM
HALF AND HALF MILK
- ESPRESSO

CAFE LATTE

MILK FOAM
STEAMED MILK
- ESPRESSO

CAPPUCCINO

MILK FOAM
STEAMED MILK
- ESPRESSO

CORRETTO

- LIQUOR
- ESPRESSO

CORTADO

- STEAMED MILK
- ESPRESSO

DOPPIO

- ESPRESSO

ESPRESSO

- ESPRESSO

ROMANO

- LEMON
- ESPRESSO

FLAT WHITE

- STEAMED MILK
- ESPRESSO

FRAPPE

WHIPPED CREAM
STEAMED MILK
- ESPRESSO

IRISH COFFEE

WHIPPED CREAM
- WHISKEY
- ESPRESSO

LATTE MACCHIATO

MILK FOAM
- ESPRESSO
STEAMED MILK

LUNGO

WATER
- ESPRESSO

MACCHIATO

MILK FOAM
- ESPRESSO

MAROCCHINO

MILK FOAM
- CHOCOLATE
- ESPRESSO

MOCHA

WHIPPED CREAM
STEAMED MILK
- CHOCOLATE
- ESPRESSO

RISTRETTO

- ESPRESSO

VIENNA

WHIPPED CREAM
- ESPRESSO

Family and Friends

I've been blessed beyond measure with a circle of friends in every city I've lived in. From growing up in Tallulah, Louisiana, to Monroe, Baton Rouge and Nashville (with brief stops in Little Rock, AR and Charleston, WV). These zip codes have allowed me to make bonds that have lasted a lifetime. So, I want to introduce you to some of my nearest and dearest and give them the opportunity to share a favorite recipe.

When I first emailed my "besties" asking for recipes, many of them replied, "You know I can't cook, so I don't have any original recipes!" I replied, "Well, you eat, don't you? Just share your favorite dish and a story to go along with it and I'll track down the recipe."

I do apologize to friends and family who are 'left out". I have dozens more people who've had an impact on my life. Please do not feel overlooked or forgotten! Especially those dear friends from high school, like Christi, Cindy, Jay, Michael, Sheri, Randy and my favorite teacher, Mrs. Pat Bray, and all those dear friends from Tallulah Academy. There were only 27 in my graduating class, so we were all close! But my publisher said at some point you just have to cut off the list. So all of my Tallulah peeps, know you definitely had an impact on my life!

Plus, I did ask more friends and family to contribute than are included here in this section of the book. But alas, they all lead very busy lives, and not everyone was able to send me their "last meal" entry or photo for this book.

Devotion

Life is richer not because of where we live, but because of who we get to walk beside along the way. Every city, every season, every chapter brings people who become part of the story God is writing through us, some for a short while and others for a lifetime. What a gift it is when God sprinkles our journey with friendships that feel like family.

These friendships do not happen by accident. They are reminders that God sees what we need before we know how to ask for it. He sends us someone to laugh with, pray with, and someone who brings comfort when the miles feel long or the days feel heavy. In His kindness, He weaves people into our lives as living expressions of His care.

And even when some relationships belong to one season and not another, none of them are wasted. God uses each connection to shape us. He softens our edges, strengthens our hearts, and teaches us love in different forms. There will always be more people who have poured into us than we could ever fit in a book, but heaven has kept the record. Not one friendship, one conversation, or one moment of grace is forgotten by God.

Some people may never make an appearance on a page, but they forever live in the heart. That is the beauty of the body of Christ: we are made to need each other, to be sharpened by each other, encouraged by each other, and carried by each other through the long miles of life.

SCRIPTURE (NIV):
"Two are better than one… If either of them falls down, one can help the other up."
— Ecclesiastes 4:9–10 (NIV)

PRAYER:
Lord, thank You for the family and friends You have placed along my path — past and present. Help me never take them for granted and teach me to be a blessing to others the way they have been a blessing to me. Knit my heart to the people You've given me and let my life always reflect gratitude for the gift of godly friendships. Amen.

Family Makes all the Difference

We'll start with family. Cause in my tribe, we put the 'fun' in dysfunctional! If I share a story about you that embarrasses you or makes you cringe, please forgive me! I've left out some of the best stories (or at least changed the names) because I never want to intentionally hurt anyone's feelings. But I decided if I was going to write about a book about my life, that some of the messy parts needed to be included. Because in the kitchen, you can't cook a meal without messing up some dishes!

To you my family: Cynthia, Stan, Larry(deceased), Sister-in-law Penney, and all the nieces and nephews: Jenny, Jill(deceased), Jason, Ashton, Cameron, Toby, Corby and all the great nieces and nephews. You have my heart. Although I've often been an "absent" aunt because of my job and having to live out of town for much of my career, it doesn't lessen the love I have for you! To my cousin Lori, who's been there through thick and thin. And to all the cousins who've spent many a holiday or family reunion with us back in the day, know that you've had an impact on me as well. Love you all.

Now, to what you're really here for in the first place. The recipes and recitations about our relationships.

Cynthia Arender Machen

My sister. Where do I start? She's six years older than me, so I was definitely the "pest" tag-along that Mama made her babysit growing up. Her nickname was "Bump". I can never remember the story of why my daddy nicknamed her that. You'll have to ask her. (My nickname was Boog, by the way. Don't know the story behind that either!) Bump was a natural in the kitchen. She could cook anything. Smoke or grill anything. We transitioned to having family get together's at her house in Tallulah after Mom and Dad passed. Not just because of the food but because we had "pickin' and grinnin" after the meal. What's a 'pickin' and grinnin'? Well, that's where my brother-in-law, Maurice Machen, would bring out his guitar and we'd sing.

My sister can sing! She can do Loretta Lynn and Tammy Wynette better than Tammy and Loretta! And by the way, Maurice, a farmer by trade, was an amazing guitar player. He used to play for Tim McGraw (before he was THE Tim McGraw) at the little country store near our farm, called Po Boy Dons. Tim even sang at Cynthia and Maurice's wedding. So Maurice would play guitar, and often our family friends, Eva Taylor Fondren would bring her keyboard, Jimmy Cook, and a smattering of other local musicians would join us. It was a hoot and holler. We'd sing until the cows came home or the neighbors complained!

Then we transitioned to karaoke. We'd gather at my sister's house or go to my cousin Lori Joyner's camp on Lake Providence, Louisiana. Truly, some of my most precious memories are of times spent eating and singing with these fine folks.

Okay, I took quite a detour from the food track, didn't I? Back to my sister's cooking. I think I looked forward to each get together for her smoked Pork Tenderloin. And I am not that huge of a pork tenderloin fan! But it was amazing, never dry. So here's that recipe! Thank you, Bump for being the best big sister I could ever have!

bottom photo: Maurice Machen, Tim McGraw, Cynthia Machen

Smoked Pork Tenderloin

2 pork tenderloins (1 lb each)
6 Tbsp butter

Brine:
¼ cup salt
2 cups water
3 Tbsp Honey

Dry Rub:
1 Tbsp Brown Sugar
1 Tbsp Paprika
1 tsp garlic powder
1 tsp onion powder
2 tsp Kosher Salt
1 tsp black pepper
½ tsp chili powder (optional)

You'll start by making the soaking solution or brine. Put the water, honey, and salt in a pot and stir over warm heat. Once everything is dissolved remove from the heat and allow to come to room temp. Soak the tenderloins for 8 to 10 hours or overnight in the fridge.

Take the pork tenderloins out of the marinade and pat dry with paper towels. You'll also want to cut off the "silverskin" from the meat. Then, take the dry rub you made and massage it onto the surface of each pork tenderloin. Then tie them together using butcher's string.

Set your smoker to 225°F. Place meat in the smoker and smoke until the internal temperature is 145°F, about 2.5 to 3 hours.

Transfer to a plate and cover with foil. Let it rest for approximately 15 to 30 minutes before slicing at a diagonal.

Devotion

Family is one of God's sweetest gifts, not because we are perfect people, but because He uses us to shape each other in ways no one else can. A sibling is often the first friend God gives us. They are the ones who know our history, our roots, our rough edges, and still chooses us through every season of life.

What a gift it is when a sibling becomes more than family, but becomes a refuge. The laughter, the music, the meals, and the memories become a kind of inheritance that is richer than anything written on paper. The world chases fame, applause, and recognition, but heaven counts love lived out in kitchens, camp houses, and late-night singing as worship.

In a culture that trades connection for convenience, true relationships are holy, living proof that God places people in our lives to anchor us, lift us, and remind us who we are when life feels scattered. Your brother or sister was not just a cook or a hostess, they were a builder of belonging.

That is the beauty of God's design. He does not just feed us through food, He feeds us through people. Through laughter, music, shared history, and shared tables. Some of the most sacred fellowship on earth happens when we gather, not because the food is perfect, but because the love is.

SCRIPTURE (NIV):
"A friend loves at all times, and a brother is born for a time of adversity." — Proverbs 17:17 (NIV)

PRAYER:
Lord, thank You for the people who have carried me, shaped me, and poured love into my life. Bless the brothers and sisters, whether by blood or by heart, who remind us of Your goodness in the everyday moments. Give me that same heart that I may love with the same warmth I've been given. Amen.

Jenny Hopkins (niece)

My nieces and nephews are my pride and joy. Since I never had children, I consider them my own. Of course, with all my living away from home and traveling for my job, I didn't get to spend as much time with them as I liked. But I always tried to make them a priority. Besides, I figured since I don't have kids, one of those nieces and nephews needs to like me enough to spoon food me or come see me in the nursing home when that time comes! So, heck yeah, I tried to butter them up!

Jenny is such an incredible woman. And that girl can cook! And she learned from the best. Her paternal grandmother, Ella Ruth Hopkins (my Mom's best friend and her maternal grandmother) was the quintessential southern cook. Her pies were perfection. Especially her chocolate pie! So I had to get that recipe. I was 19 years old, I think, when my sister Cynthia announced she and her first husband, John Hopkins, were a having a child. I was still just a kid myself. And had pretty much been the "baby" of the family and the center of everyone's universe, lol, when this little bundle of joy entered our lives. And what a joy she has been.

She has been a 'giver' from the start. Always thinking of others. And boy, did she become a great mom to my super niece Ella (I call her super instead of great, because great niece makes me sound ancient!). In Jenny's case, my mother was her maternal grandmother and her father's mother, Ella Ruth Hopkins, was my mom's best friend. Even after my mom and dad divorced and my parents passed, Ella Ruth was such a precious part of my life. She would listen with compassion and empathy when I wanted to talk about boys or family drama. I loved that woman as much as my own grandmother. And Jenny did too! We cried a river of tears when sweet Ella Ruth went on to glory. Jenny and I agreed that this cookbook would not be complete without Ella Ruth's chocolate pie.

Devotion

Some of the sweetest blessings in life are not things we build with our own hands, but relationships we inherit through the love of others. The kitchen to me became a place where love was taught, character was shaped, and where faithfulness was passed down one pie crust at a time.

Family is not just biology; it is investment. It is presence. It is the imprint of love that lingers even when a voice goes silent. The best cooks in our lives rarely set out to impress us, but they simply fed us while they were loving us. Long after the meal is gone, the memory remains, because what nourished us went deeper than the plate.

You may not have had children of your own, but you have mothered through your love, your laughter, your encouragement, your presence, and your open heart. Spiritual motherhood is every bit as real, and often just as needed, as biological motherhood. God never wastes the love we pour out, and He does not measure parenthood by bloodline.

We can plant seeds that grow long after we are gone. This is the miracle of God's design: love multiplies through generations, not because we are perfect, but because we show up, and because we pour into others, the way someone once poured into us.

SCRIPTURE (NIV):
"One generation commends Your works to another; they tell of Your mighty acts."
— Psalm 145:4

PRAYER:

Lord, thank You for the women who shaped us, fed us, and loved us into who we are, whether that be mothers by birth, by heart, or by faith. Help me carry their legacy well and continue planting seeds of kindness, generosity, and love into the next generation. Let my life be a reminder that spiritual family is a gift and love never dies. Amen.

Ella Ruth's
Chocolate Cream Pie

2 squares unsweetened chocolate
1⅓ cups sugar
¾ cup flour
2 ⅔ cup milk
4 eggs, separated
1 tsp vanilla
1 ½ cups pecans, finely chopped

Melt the chocolate in the top of double boiler. Add sugar, flour, salt and milk. Mix well over medium heat. You'll need to stir constantly. The mixture will start to get thick.

Next, you'll add the eggs but you'll need to temper them. That means adding a little bit of the hot chocolate mixture to the egg yolks while whisking. This way you won't have scrambled eggs.

Add that mixture back to the chocolate and cook for another 3 minutes.

Remove from the heat and add your butter and vanilla. Pour into a baked 9" pie shell. You can use the egg whites to make a meringue, although I don't recall Ella Ruth putting a meringue on top.

Ashton Machen (niece)

Then there's my niece Ashton! What a firecracker. Smart as whip. Valedictorian of her class. She's charting her own course in so many ways. I am loving being her cheerleader on the sidelines of her life. I lived away in either Baton Rouge or Nashville during her growing-up years. But when I would come home, I'd always try to spend time with her. She got her pharmacy degree from my alma mater, the University of Louisiana-Monroe. I do remember her telling me a couple of years before she graduated that she didn't think she would be happy as a pharmacist. But I begged her to continue on that degree path. She was four years into this grueling degree program, and I felt like she could write her ticket if she got the degree. Even if she didn't want to be a pharmacist. I've always regretted telling her to stay the course. She's not been happy as a pharmacist. I didn't realize, and she didn't either initially, that she really wanted to be a farmer! Yep, a hands-in-the-dirt-making-things-grow, farmer, just like her father and grandfather— my dad! I'm still praying that she can do that. We need someone in our family to carry on the agricultural legacy!

After Ashton became an adult, I soon learned that she shared my love of cooking. She would ask for a recipe or text me and ask how to cook this or that. She even came to visit me one weekend when I was living in Charleston, West Virginia. I asked what she wanted do while here. I assumed she would want to sightsee since it was part of the country that she'd never seen before. She said, let's cook! So we did. I had just put some tweaks on a pasta recipe, and it was so darn good. She said, let's make that! So here it is. Love you more than my Kitchen Aid mixer, Ashton! Now, go forth and farm!

Devotion

One of the hardest lessons we learn in life is that the path that looks wise in human eyes is not always the one that brings joy to the soul. We grow up hearing "stay the course," "finish what you start," and "choose the secure route," but God often writes His plans in places the world overlooks, like a field, a farm, a seed, or a dream that looks "unusual" from the outside.

Sometimes the people we love most are the ones we unintentionally nudge toward safety instead of purpose. Not out of selfishness, but out of protection. We want them to have something steady and respectable. However, God wants them to have something fulfilling and eternal. There is a sacred kind of courage required to let a person become fully who God designed them to be, even when the journey doesn't match our expectations.

What a beautiful thing it is when someone circles back later in life and discovers that their heart still beats in rhythm with their roots. That longing is not random; it is inheritance. It is God tugging us toward the place where our spirit feels most alive.

The world tells us to "make something of ourselves." God tells us to become who He made us to be. Those are two very different things.

And the Lord is patient. He wastes no detour, no degree, and no delay. Every step, even the ones that weren't "the one," prepares us for the moment our calling finds its voice. Where we end up will be in God's hands, but our desire to grow things is already a reflection of His creativity.

The same God who authored our gifts will finish the story He started in all of us.

SCRIPTURE (NIV):
"In their hearts humans plan their course, but the Lord establishes their steps."
— Proverbs 16:9

PRAYER:
Lord, thank You for the callings You place within us — the ones that whisper before they roar. Help us support the dreams of the people we love, even when their path looks different than we imagined. Give us courage to walk in the purpose You planted in us, and give us all hearts willing to follow wherever You lead. Amen.

Chicken and Sausage Linguine Casserole

Pasta:
8 oz. pasta
1 Tbsp salt
1 Tbsp olive oil

Meats:
3 Tbsp butter
   unsalted and divided
1 lb chicken breast
6 oz smoked sausage
   sliced to ¼" pieces
8 oz baby Bella mushrooms
   sliced
Cajun seasoning to taste
Italian seasoning to taste
Salt and pepper

Sauce:
4 cloves garlic
   minced
1 cup chicken broth
1 Tbsp Worcestershire sauce
1 cup heavy cream
2 tsp Cajun seasoning
1 tsp Paprika
½ tsp garlic powder
¾ cup Parmesan cheese
   freshly grated
sea salt to taste

Pasta:

To a large pot of boiling water, add a tablespoon of salt and a tablespoon of olive oil. Cook pasta according to the package instructions. Drain and set.

Meats:

It's always a good idea to pat your chicken dry with paper towels. Then sprinkle with salt, pepper, Cajun and Italian seasonings. You're going cook these whole. We'll slice later.

Next, slice your sausage into ¼-inch circles and slice mushrooms.

I use my largest skillet for this. Put in your 1 tablespoon of butter and melt it over medium-high heat. Next, add your whole chicken breasts. Cook for about 4 to 5 minutes on each side. Remove chicken, and now you can slice into bite-size pieces.

Next, brown your sliced sausage. Cook them on medium heat for 2-3 minutes on each side until darker in color around the edges. Remove.

I like to deglaze the skillet with a splash of water or chicken stock. Then, add the other tablespoon of butter and sliced mushrooms. Sometimes I add more butter. Just eyeball it. You can also add some olive oil if you like. Sauté the mushrooms. Once cooked, remove them from the skillet as well.

Sauce:

Add remaining butter, allow it to melt and then cook garlic in it until slightly browned, being careful not to burn. Add the chicken broth, Worcestershire and heavy cream. Bring to a light simmer before adding your Cajun seasoning, paprika and garlic powder. Then, whisk it all in.

Last, add the Parmesan cheese and whisk to blend for 2 to 3 minutes to thicken the sauce. Taste the sauce and add salt to taste.

Now it's time to add the cooked pasta and mix well. Next, add the chicken, sausage and mushrooms back into the pan and allow them to reheat for 2 to 3 minutes.

Jason Whitaker (nephew)

I've mentioned that I consider my nieces and nephews my children since I have no kids of my own. My nephew Jason has had quite an impact on my life and on the lives of others. And he probably doesn't even realize it. To watch his journey has been so inspirational. I won't share his entire personal story because it's not mine to share. But he has overcome so much. Been through hell and back but is such a bright light now in everyone's life. He is now pouring into the lives of others. His path has had so many twists, turns, and rough patches. But whose journey hasn't, right? I'll let him share all the details, but know this: he's a shining example of no matter how many demons you try to wrestle to the ground, it's next to impossible to do in your own strength. But our God is greater! You WILL overcome! Jason has a heart the size of Texas. It's been a joy and privilege to watch him turn his life around and become a person who is so giving

and willing to offer a helping hand to anyone, day or night! Love you, Jason (or as Daddy used to call you, Jacob! Lol and we never knew why!)

Jason's contributing his BLT dip!

"With men this is impossible, but with God all things are possible." —Matthew 19:26

Jason's BLT Dip

1 lb bacon
1 cup mayonnaise
1 cup sour cream
1 tomato, diced

Place bacon in a large skillet and cook over medium-high heat, turning occasionally, until evenly browned, about 10 minutes. Drain bacon slices on paper towels (you can use packaged cooked real bacon bits).

Combine mayonnaise and sour cream in a medium bowl. Crumble bacon into mayonnaise mixture; mix until combined. Stir in tomatoes right before serving.

Use Frito scoops, your favorite chip or vegetable for dipping and enjoy.

Devotion

Some testimonies are loud from the beginning, polished, steady, and straight-line journeys of faith. But others rise slowly, like a sunrise after a long night, and those are often the most powerful because they carry proof of what God can redeem. Watching someone walk through darkness and learn how to stand again reminds us that grace does not just forgive. it restores.

Our breakthrough is not about never falling, but about finally learning Who to lean on when we do. We can exhaust ourselves trying to win battles in our own strength, but some victories are only born when we finally surrender and let God take the lead. The enemy loves to use shame to convince us that our past defines us, but God uses testimony to remind us that our past prepared us.

There is nothing more beautiful than watching someone discover that the same place they once struggled is now the place they can minister from. Brokenness becomes compassion. Pain becomes perspective. A scar becomes a map someone else can follow. That is how God turns a survivor into a servant.

The world loves a success story, but heaven celebrates a redemption story; the kind where God gets the glory because He was the only One strong enough to lift a life out of the pit and place it on solid ground. We are all walking proof that God does not just give second chances; He gives new beginnings.

SCRIPTURE (NIV):
"Jesus looked at them and said, 'With man this is impossible, but with God all things are possible.'" — Matthew 19:26

"You are from God and have overcome them, for he who is in you is greater than he who is in the world." — 1 John 4:4

PRAYER:
Lord, thank You for being stronger than our weakness, greater than our past, and faithful through every chapter of our story. Bless us and the testimony we carry and use our lives as a beacon of hope for others still fighting their battles. Teach me to rely on Your strength instead of my own, and to believe that no life is ever too far gone for Your redemption. Amen.

Cameron "Tank" Machen

My nephew Cameron. God truly broke the mold when He made you! If you meet Cameron, you love him. He's funny, smart, and a unique human being. He got the nickname "Tank" in high school. He was a machine on the football field, an army tank. We were all so proud when he announced he'd be going into the ministry. He decided to go to New Orleans Theological Seminary to become a youth pastor. He has such a passion for influencing young people and pointing them to Jesus. His sense of humor, his gift for speaking and his love for others just blow me away. He also has a passion for cooking "meat." And since I don't cook a lot of meat, I was thrilled when he wanted to contribute this dish to the cookbook. It's actually something I've never heard of!

Love you to the beach and back, Cam-bone!

Devotion

We see people who carry the kind of joy that tells you God did something intentional when He made them. They walk into a room and instantly lift it, not because they try, but because their spirit overflows. That is what it looks like when a calling fits a person's design and their heart line up with God's purpose for their life.

Ministry is not just a pulpit, sometimes it is laughter, or presence, or simply being someone young people can trust. There is something beautiful about watching God redirect a fighter's spirit into becoming a spiritual protector.

It's such a picture of who He is: steady, substantial, something that fills and strengthens us. Some people feed bodies, some people feed souls, and some do both. Youth today are hungry for authenticity, not polish. They do not need perfect leaders, just real ones. Leaders who love Jesus out loud and live it with a whole heart.

All of our lives are proof that God equips those He calls. When someone steps into the role heaven wrote for them, there is a grace about them that you can feel even before you understand it. That is God's anointing.

SCRIPTURE (NIV):
"Whatever you do, work at it with all your heart, as working for the Lord, not for human masters."
— Colossians 3:23

PRAYER:
Lord, thank You for the way You call each of us uniquely. Bless all of those who pour into the next generation with joy and authenticity. Strengthen their ministry, deepen their roots, and use their life as a reminder that service done with love is worship. Help us all to walk boldly in the calling You crafted for us. Amen.

Smoked Picanha Roast

1 Picanha Roast

Rub:
½ cup black pepper
⅓ cup garlic powder
⅓ cup kosher salt
½ cup yellow mustard (optional)

The first step is to find a picanha roast. That might not be the easiest step, however, because not every grocery store has picanha ready to go. But if you get to know the local butcher or the manager of your favorite store's meat department, they should be able to help you. You might even find it by another name, because the picanha is really only the Portuguese nickname. It's no wonder I have grown to love this cut, as a man who also more widely known by a nickname. It's true name is the coulotte muscle or the sirloin cap, as it is the "cap" that sits on top of the sirloin. Though it is a fairly underused cut, it has been popularized by the Brazilian churrascarias hence the Portuguese nickname. Hopefully, you have made friends with the butcher, and he can do the minimal trimming the roast requires. If not, don't worry; it's not that hard. There may be just a bit of silver skin on the bottom, and you can trim the fat cap on top to your desired thickness. (Personally, I love the fat. It's why I love this roast. So, I trim almost none.) That's it.

Now that you have your trimmed and ready picanha roast home, you will want to take it out and pat it dry. Then, to the dry surface, you will want to apply a rub consisting of salt, pepper and garlic powder. I find keeping the rub simple usually produces a better result. You can tweak the rub to add flavors that you like but I would be careful not to add too much sugar or large bits that will simply burn during the cooking process. Whatever you choose to use as your rub, apply it to the roast liberally! Once you have applied this rub, you want to let the roast sit for at least an hour or longer. This is called a "dry brine." This process will draw out moisture and ensure that you will get a beautiful dark bark by the end. You can let it sit in the refrigerator if you would like, but you will need to let the roast get back to room temperature before cooking.

Letting the "dry brine" is doing its thing will give you some time to setup your smoker. You do not need a huge smoker because most picanha roasts are only between 2.5-5 pounds. So your small pellet smoker, or Weber Kettle (this is your quintessential BBQ grill. You know the one.) will be perfect. Do whatever prep your smoker takes to get to 275°F. Once you have a consistent 275°F, you are ready to put in your room temperature picanha roast.

The rest of the cook is mostly just waiting. You're looking at approximately an hour of smoke time per pound of your roast. However, internal temperature is much more important than cook time. I personally would not suggest trying this without a instant-read meat thermometer that you trust. What will make this even easier is if you have a temperature probe that can monitor the internal temperature of your roast without your opening your smoker. This will cut down on how many times you open the smoker to check the

temp and inadvertently release all of that beautiful, delicious smoke and lower the temperature inside your grill. The internal temperature that you are looking for is dependent on your personal preference. I prefer a medium-rare steak, so I prefer a medium-rare roast. I pull my roast once it has hit 130 degrees. If you like your steak a little more well-done you can wait until 140-150°F internally.

The final step is important and can be the most difficult. You have to wait. I know that bark is going to be barking and your mouth is going to be watering, but like any steak, you have to let it rest at least 20 minutes. This allows the natural juices of the roast to redistribute and will save your roast from being

dried out in the long run. Once you are ready to cut the roast, there is another equally important rule. You must cut against the grain of the roast. If you don't know what that means, ask your butcher friend before you leave the store. There will be a very noticeable difference in tenderness if you cut it incorrectly.

The last step is the most important one. Gather your best friends and enjoy a delicious roast together. I personally like to cut it into long, thin strips and dip it in my favorite steak or BBQ sauce. Others may prefer to eat without sauce (I don't know why, I am a sauce person) or even a chimichurri. However you like yours, enjoy it with those you love.

Lori Joyner (cousin)

There's nothing like a cousin connection. My cousin, Lori Joyner, became like a sister to me in our early adult years. She's my daddy's niece's daughter. Her grandmother Ulma Clement was Daddy's sister. I think we were destined to be close because her dad was also named Billy Ray! And her mom, Carolyn, was like a second mother to me.

Lori and I have had some adventures. From heading out to Dallas to see the famous "Southfork Ranch" from the TV show Dallas(from the '80s) to snow ski trips in Colorado, and many a 'pickin and grinnin' at her camp on Lake Providence, La. We have laughed, cried, and drove many a man crazy with our personalities and passion for life. Lori is a retired schoolteacher. She has impacted more young people in a positive way and set them on a path for success than anyone I know. She took her job very seriously. She made sure that every student was seen, heard, and nurtured to be everything they could be. Even if they had learning disabilities. Especially, if they had learning disabilities. Not a single child was going to go unnoticed on her watch.

Besides being a great teacher, she's also a great tractor and U-Haul truck driver! She's been there to help me in my many moves from Tennessee and Louisiana. I've moved so much that people think I'm running from the law! Lori has been at the ready to drive that U-Haul truck at the drop of a hat! So thank you, Lori, for being more than a cousin, a true-blue friend. Love you Big!

Her recipe is a fabulous Fudge Pie. So easy yet so good.

Lori's Fudge Pie

3 eggs
1 cup sugar
⅓ cup butter, melted
4 Tbsp cocoa

1 can condensed milk
1 tsp vanilla
1 unbaked pie shell (9" deep dish)

Combine all ingredients. Pour into the unbaked pie shell and bake for 35 minutes at 350°F.

Devotion

We see people who carry the kind of joy that tells you God did something intentional when There are people God places in our lives who become anchors. Cousins can turn into confidants, friends can turn into family, and shared history can deepen into a bond that feels God-ordained. You don't always get to choose who you're related to, but sometimes God gifts you with someone who feels chosen to walk beside you through seasons that require more than a bloodline.

What stands out about friendship is consistently showing up. In a world full of disappearing acts, people who keep showing up are holy gifts. They are the ones who stay for the laughter and the moving trucks, who help not only pack your boxes, but your burdens. They are proof that love is a verb long before it is a feeling.

The Kingdom of God is built not only through preachers and pastors, but through teachers and servants, through quiet encouragers and loyal friends who show Christ without ever holding a microphone.

Some people impact the world by reaching thousands. Others impact the world by loving deeply… one life at a time. Heaven keeps the record of every unseen act of service, every mile driven out of love, every silent rescue no one else knew about.

True friendship is not just companionship; it is God's tenderness wrapped in human skin.

SCRIPTURE (NIV):
"Carry each other's burdens, and in this way you will fulfill the law of Christ."
— Galatians 6:2

PRAYER:
Lord, thank You for the people who show love not just in words, but in their willingness to walk beside us through every season. Bless those who serve quietly, faithfully, joyfully, and lift us when life feels heavy. Help me to be that kind of person to others, reflecting Your heart through loyalty and love. Amen.

Penney Cobb Wilkins (sister-in-law)

I may have mentioned my mom had two boys when she was married to Hubert Wilkins, prior to marrying my dad. Her youngest son was Larry. I don't have many memories of him because of our age gap. But I do remember him being a good-looking fella. He had eyelashes that would make Elizabeth Taylor jealous. I just love the photo of him and his son Toby. The classic car. The cool look. He and Penney Cobb fell in love. This is Hallmark movie kind of love. There was no doubt these two were soulmates. They made a stunning couple. My sweet brother Larry had his share of demons, though. I don't think Penney will mind my sharing his story. Larry battled drug and alcohol addiction. At the young age of 38, he died. It was heartbreaking. He was so young. His kids were very young. Toby and Corby lost their dad. Penney lost the love of her life. But here's what I want you to remember about Larry. Not that he had a drinking problem, but he had a passion for life. He knew life was too short not to laugh, not to love with reckless abandon and not share life, even the messy and "not living up to expectations of those you love" life. That's what's called family. We loved Larry to the moon and back. It's a reminder that in God's family, He takes us as we are. Warts and all!

We all have our "stuff." We all have something in our lives that can take us over if we're not careful. But part of the reason I wanted to write this book, not just as a cookbook, is to let you know you can overcome! Ask for help. Seek Jesus. So many of us look to food, drugs, drink, and sex to fill a void. Just to feel something. But until you realize that the hole in your heart can only be filled by Jesus and not another pill or pint, you'll never be whole. You'll never have peace. It's not too late, and you're not too far gone. Larry's life was cut short. He never got to know Toby and Corby's beautiful children. That breaks my heart.

So know this, whatever you're battling today, God will provide a way out. It's hard to see because addictions are all-consuming. There's physical pain and mental anguish when you're in the throes of addiction. But I promise you, God is a chain breaker and way maker! It's not a willpower thing, it's a Jesus thing!

One thing I remember eating at Penney's house was her amazing sweet potato casserole. Which is basically a traditional southern recipe, but she must have used an extra cup of love because hers was always the best!

Devotion

Grief is never simple when it touches someone we love, especially when their life carried both beauty and brokenness. But we are not defined by our struggle, we are defined by our heart. That is what love chooses to remember. Addiction may have marked you or someone you love, but it does not erase worth.

We all carry something that tries to wear us down, maybe not addiction in the obvious sense, but pain we try to numb, fear we try to quiet, or emptiness we try to fill. Some people's battles show on the outside, and others fight wars quietly where nobody sees. Still, every single one of us is in need of rescue.

The enemy always tells us we are too far gone. Jesus always says, "Come home."

The enemy shames. Jesus restores.

The enemy chains. Jesus sets free.

Addiction does not make someone weak, it means they were carrying something too heavy for one soul to hold alone. But God does not meet us at the finish line when we are cleaned up. Instead, He sits with us in the ashes and says, "I won't leave you here."

Those stories o addiction are reminders that life is fragile, time is short, and healing is urgent. Freedom is not impossible. But it does not begin with trying harder, it begins with turning toward the One who breaks chains by touching the heart before touching the habit.

If you are fighting something in the dark today, hear this with your whole soul:

You are not beyond reach. You are not beyond mercy. You are not beyond new beginnings.

Jesus does not shame you for the battle, He offers you strength in it.

SCRIPTURE (NIV):
"It is for freedom that Christ has set us free. Stand firm, then, and do not let yourselves be burdened again by a yoke of slavery."
— Galatians 5:1

"I can do all things through him who strengthens me."
— Philippians 4:13

PRAYER:
Jesus, thank You for loving us in our weakness as much as in our strength. For anyone who is battling silently, give them courage to reach for You. Break every chain that tries to claim their life, and remind them that Your grace is greater than their struggle. Heal hearts, restore hope, and breathe freedom into every place that feels impossible. Lord, help me with the things I battle and remind me that with you, all things are possible. Amen.

Sweet Potato Casserole

Casserole:

3 cups cold sweet potatoes, mashed
    (prepared without milk or butter)

1 cup sugar

3 large eggs

½ cup whole milk
    (sometimes I use heavy cream)

¼ cup butter, melted

1 tsp salt

1 tsp vanilla extract

Topping:

½ cup brown sugar, packed

½ cup pecans, chopped

¼ cup all-purpose flour

4 Tbsp butter, cold

Start by peeling the sweet potatoes. Cut them into 1-to-2-inch cubes. Try to keep them as close to the same size as possible so they'll cook evenly. Bring to a rolling boil. Cook for about 12 to 15 minutes. Rinse and drain.

Preheat oven to 325°F.

Using a hand mixer, beat the sweet potatoes, sugar, eggs, milk, butter, salt and vanilla until smooth. In a large bowl. Transfer to a greased 2-qt. baking dish.

In a small bowl, combine the brown sugar, pecans and flour; cut in butter until crumbly. Sprinkle over the sweet potato mixture. Bake, uncovered, until a thermometer reads 160°F, 45 to 50 minutes.

Tammi's tip for potatoes: Always start with cold water! This helps cook the potatoes evenly from the inside out.

Cup of Comfort

There's a quiet moment that comes after giving to others; after the meals are made, the needs are met, and the house finally exhales. The coffee has gone cold, the lists are mostly done, and you feel the gentle pull of exhaustion settle in. For caregivers, nurturers, and everyday givers of love, this moment is familiar. It's the pause after pouring yourself out all day, when your heart whispers, "I need a refill."

No one can keep pouring endlessly. Even the most giving soul runs dry if they never stop to refill itself. Just as a cup can't pour from emptiness, a heart can't give joy when it's completely spent. That's where the practice of small, steady comfort comes in to remind you that your well-being matters, too.

The Ritual of Refilling

Self-care doesn't always look like a weekend away or an afternoon at the spa. It is often the smallest moments that quietly restore peace to your day. Taking it slow, like sipping tea at dawn, seeing the sunrise on a walk, or jotting down thoughts to clear your head, might seem small. However, they are each filling your cup.

Small Daily Rituals That Make a Big Difference

Create Something. Doing the things we like, such as creating a painting, writing a poem, or making a new flower arrangement, can help fill our cup with joy.

Write Without Pressure. Journaling doesn't have to be perfect, pretty, or lengthy. Some days it's a prayer, other days it's a list of things you're grateful for, one day it was the simply a note to myself: "Today was hard." Your journal becomes a mirror of grace for yourself.

Take a Walk. Moving your body outdoors is one of the simplest ways to reset your mind. While it still requires effort and energy, if you focus on things such as the wind, the sky, the sound of nature, each step can be a small step of release.

End the Day Well. Light a candle, dim the lights, read a few words from a book or listen to your favorite podcast before bed. Let the day close in peace instead of noise. An enjoyable ending helps your spirit begin again stronger the next day.

Why Refilling Is Holy Work

Pouring into others is sacred, but letting yourself be poured into is also. When you refill, you honor the same vessel that God uses to serve others. You give yourself permission to receive comfort as deeply as you give it.

Look at your "cup of comfort" as spiritual maintenance. It's how you keep showing up with love instead of fatigue, compassion instead of resentment. None of us can run for long on empty because we are meant to have a cup that overflows.

So tonight, before you tend to one more task for others, ask yourself, "What fills me?" Then, do one small thing to honor that answer.

Stan Wilkins

My brother Stan is my half-brother. I share a mom with. Mom was married to Mr. Wilkins before she married my dad. By the time Mom married Daddy, and had Cynthia and me, Stan and Larry were out of the house. Stan and I became close after I became an adult. He was the academic in the family. I mean crazy smart. He got his undergraduate degree at Louisiana Tech in Ruston. He was a Tech Bulldog and played on the same field, during the same time, I think, as Terry Bradshaw and Phil Robertson. If you're not familiar with Phil Robertson, of Duck Dynasty fame, you may not know the story. (Google Phil Robertson of Duck Dynasty)

Phil Robertson was the starting quarterback at La Tech but quit after one season when he realized playing college football would interfere with his duck hunting! So Phil quit playing college football and started his very own duck-calling business. Terry Bradshaw, the backup quarterback at the time, became the starting quarterback for La Tech. The rest, as they say... Bradshaw became the QB for the Pittsburgh Steelers and eventually a Hall of Fame NFL quarterback. Robertson became the patriarch of the popular reality TV show, Duck Dynasty. Now back to my brother Stan. He didn't play football. But he played the trumpet! So, Stan was playing in the band at halftime when these greats were playing football! (I said he was playing on the same field; he just wasn't playing football!) So technically they all "played" on the same field. I just love telling that story. Stan went on to get his doctorate from LSU. He loved teaching and eventually became the vice chancellor of Bossier Community College in Bossier City, Louisiana. Stan not only has book smarts, but he knows his way around the kitchen. We alternate going to his house out in the country in Plain Dealing, La for holiday get togethers. We look so forward to his cheesy spaghetti and homemade yeast rolls! Oh, those rolls (see page 20 for yeast rolls recipe).

(And keep reading for a Cheesy Spaghetti recipe. My friend Lisa Boullt also submitted a cheesy spaghetti recipe, and I tried not to duplicate recipes.)

Devotion

Every family carries different strengths, and one of the ways God shows His creativity is through the variety of gifts He spreads among us. Some people influence the world through a platform, others through a pulpit, and still others through a classroom, a kitchen, or a quiet, steady life of faithfulness. The world tends to notice the loudest voices, but heaven keeps careful record of the faithful ones.

Wisdom is not just what we know, it is how we use what we've been given. Teaching is one of the most Christlike callings a person can carry, because it plants seeds that grow long after the moment has passed. You don't always see fruit right away, but you know you've poured into something eternal.

God gives each of us a role in His Kingdom family, and not one calling is greater than another. The preacher needs the teacher. The encourager needs the mentor. The family needs the steady soul who shows up year after year, bringing wisdom, warmth, and stability. It is not always the voices in the spotlight that shape us most deeply. Sometimes it is the ones who sit across the table and live their faith one ordinary day at a time.

SCRIPTURE (NIV):
"Do not despise these small beginnings, for the Lord rejoices to see the work begin."
— Zechariah 4:10

PRAYER:
Lord, thank You for the people in our lives whose steady faithfulness has shaped us more than they know. Help me honor the quiet callings as much as the visible ones and remind me that every gift You give has purpose. Teach me to celebrate the unique design You've placed in each of us, and to use mine for Your glory. Amen.

Sweet Tea Collard Greens

3 lb fresh collard greens
5 strips of bacon
½ cup sweet onion
1 ham hock
1 Tbsp sugar
½ Tbsp garlic powder
⅓ cup apple cider vinegar
1 Tbsp olive oil

Start with a large pot over medium and put in the olive oil. Add the bacon and chopped onion and cook until bacon is done. Add the sweet tea and ham hock. Followed by the apple cider vinegar, sugar, garlic powder and stir well.

Now, add in the chopped collards and make sure they're all submerged.

Bring to a boil. Cover and reduce to a simmer for 1.5 to 2 hours. When greens are tender, remove the ham hock and chop up the meat and add back to the greens if you desire.

Lauren Kitchens Steward

If there was ever a friend who God intentionally put in my path to be a forever friend and prayer partner, is Lauren Kitchens Steward. From the very beginning, this friendship was divine intervention. Let me tell you our amazing story!

I was working as the weekend news anchor at WKRN in Nashville in 1995. I was probably the only woman on the planet who did not like to shop. I hated going to the mall (still do). But my news director begged me one day to please use the clothing allowance the station provided to buy some new clothes. My wardrobe was so outdated it looked like I was zooming into the 80s. So, I forced myself to go to the mall in West Nashville. I just happened to walk into a clothing store called Gantos. Had never heard of it before or since. As I'm forcing myself to shop for "anchor" worthy clothes, this beautiful, striking and very kind woman asked if she could help me. Her name was Lauren. She and I immediately hit it off. We talked and chatted as if we were lifelong friends. She was from Tupelo, Mississippi. When I asked what brought her to Nashville, she said she moved here to get a job in radio or TV. She was a dedicated Christian and really wanted to do Christian radio. At the time, I was working fulltime at News 2 but I was also part-time at a local "oldies format" radio station. I was doing their morning news. Ironically, I was about to take vacation and the GM at the radio station asked me to find someone who could fill in for me while I was gone

that week. I asked Lauren if she wanted to do that. She said yes, even though it was secular radio and it was news. But it was an open door.

And to hear Lauren tell the story, the week she was on the air, she said she was a tongue-tied disaster on air. She said she mispronounced words, didn't get along with the DJ, and wasn't familiar with any of the songs. But God was all over it. God's timing is everything. For just a split second, someone from one of the Nashville Christian radio stations just happened to hear Lauren when she was on the air. And guess what? Lauren ended up getting a job offer at the Christian station in Nashville, which ended up leading to a job offer in the biggest radio/TV market in the country! Los Angeles!!! It just goes to show that God can open doors in ways you least expect it; when you least expect it. But the best part is she's been my bestie ever since that first day in Gantos in the late 90s. She has listened to me whine for hours on end about men, bosses, family, finances, and frustrating situations. To this day, no matter how far apart we've lived from each other, she's my go-to. Thank you, God, for bringing Lauren into my life. And thank you, Lauren, for being one who sticks closer than a brother!

Lauren is sharing her husband's Sweet Tea Collard greens (previous pages) and her dad's banana pudding recipes. (pages 104-105) Lauren admits she can barely boil water!

Devotion

There are some friendships that heaven hand-delivers. Sometimes the Lord answers a prayer we never even thought to pray by placing the right person beside us at exactly the right moment. Not a coincidence, but a calling.

What makes this friendship so special is not just how it began, but what it became. God often places people in our path not just to bless us at the moment, but to walk with us through decades of storms, laughter, waiting, and prayer. These are the friendships that become spiritual shelter.

God opens doors in ways we never could orchestrate. God is not limited by the setting, the format, the timing, or the path. When He wants to position someone, even a stumble can become a step forward.

When God assigns a friend to your life, geography doesn't weaken the bond and time doesn't dilute the call. Prayer threads hearts together more tightly than proximity ever could. These are the friendships that hold you together when you feel undone, that listen when you're empty, and that speak Jesus when you forget how to.

SCRIPTURE (NIV):
"Love each other as I have loved you. Greater love has no one than this: to lay down one's life for one's friends." — John 15:12-13

PRAYER:
Lord, thank You for the ones You send by Your own design. People who speak life, walk with us in prayer, and reflect Your heart to us. Bless them with loyalty and love that only You can give. Help me to recognize and honor You in being one of those people for someone else. Amen.

Banana Pudding

14 oz. can sweetened condensed milk

1 ⅓ cups whole milk

5.1 oz. package instant vanilla pudding mix

1 tub of Cool Whip

1 tsp pure vanilla extract

12 oz. box vanilla wafer cookies

4 bananas, sliced into coins

To be honest, Bill Kitchens recipe didn't include using condensed milk. But this was so close to my mom's recipe that I decided to throw it in! So, start by whisking condensed milk, whole milk, vanilla and pudding mix together. Make sure there are no lumps. Refrigerate until set, about 5 minutes.

Fold in Cool Whip whipped cream into pudding mixture.

Now for assembly. Cover the bottom of your dish with vanilla wafers. Followed by bananas. Top with one-third of the pudding mixture. Repeat until you reach the top, ending with a final layer of pudding. Set aside the remaining wafers for serving.

Refrigerate for at least 3 hours or up to overnight. Just before serving, add crumbled vanilla wafers to the top and more Cool Whip if you have any!

Crazy Small World

Okay, here's another coinki-dink story involving Lauren. Several months into our friendship, I walked into Lauren's apartment in Brentwood, TN and stopped to look at all the framed pictures. This woman had a ministry at one time of taking photos and having them printed out and framed. Remember that? Before we all kept photos on our phones! As I'm perusing the pictures, I notice this beautiful short-haired redhead standing next to Lauren in a photo. I said, "Wow, that looks like one of my best friends, Jane Prater." Lauren looked at me and said, "that's one of my friends from Ole Miss, Jane Prater!" I couldn't believe it. I worked with Jane at KTVE in Monroe, Louisiana probably 8 or 9 years earlier. Jane was a news producer. She was behind the scenes. I was an anchor, along with Kriss Fairbairn. Lauren and I immediately called Jane and said, "You're not going to believe who my new BFF is!!" Such a small world.

Now on to my friends, Jane Prater Yerger and Kriss Fairbairn Fortunato.

When I started my TV career in Monroe, Louisiana, I met people who are still dear friends today. From those early days at KNOE and KTVE, I have stayed in contact with several of them. Judy, Angie, Devon, and several more from KNOE.

At KTVE, I worked with Kriss Fairbairn Fortunato and Jane Prater Yerger. We were the three musketeers! And let me just say, we were young (and those two were knockouts!) and ready to take on the world. We were also a bit boy crazy. I swear, I think Jane and I chased after the University of Louisiana-Monroe football players so hard that many of them got recruited for the Track team! There are several stories I could share here, but I'll refrain.

Jane was responsible for putting the newscasts together that Kriss and I anchored. While Jane was good at producing, she soon learned she really didn't enjoy it. So she quit the TV news business, left Monroe and went to paralegal school. She returned to her home state of Alabama. What many people don't know about Jane is that she is an incredible singer. I think Jane could have pursued a music career. (Oh, I don't think I mentioned that Lauren is also an incredible singer! That's how she and Jane became good friends. They were in a musical group at Ole Miss.)

So when I moved to Nashville, not to be a country music singer but cover and report on the country music industry, I told Jane she should move to Nashville! She did! We would hang out at the Longhorn Steakhouse near Music Row and talk with all these up-and-coming singer/songwriters, like Kenny Chesney, Wade Hayes, Chris Cagle, Billy Ray Cyrus, etc. Remember, I said, "up and coming, these guys were just starting out. I think Kenny Chesney was the only one who actually had a song on the radio at the time, but he was far from stardom then.

Then one day, after a weekend trip back home to Alabama, Jane walked into the apartment and said, "I've met the man I'm going to marry." I'm like, "What?!" She said, "I saw Frank Yerger, our eyes met across the room, and I knew he's the one." And sure as shootin' they got married, have three beautiful children and live in Oxford, MS. Such an incredible love story.

Jane, Kriss, and I can go months without talking, but we always know we're there for each other. We call each other the "birdheads". A little inside joke that I'll save for another book. Jane and Kriss both have

been a rock for me. Always so wise. Always thoughtful. But, most importantly, always speaks the truth to me. Even when it may not be what I want to hear. That's a true friend!! We may no longer be the three musketeers, but we have a bond and connection that will never be broken. I love those ladies. Thank you for being forever friends!

Jane chose to share with me her mom's chocolate cake recipe. This is one of those family recipes that Jane says was kept under lock and key. It was never "shared," only passed down to a trusted family member. But Jane said her mother gave her permission to share the recipe not too long before she passed. I sure loved Mrs. Joyce Prater (and her husband Harlan). I never had her chocolate cake, but now that I know how to make it, it's become one of those indulgent treats that satisfies a chocolate craving like nothing else!

Joyce's Flourless Chocolate Cake (AKA "Death By Chocolate" in the Prater family)

1 lb butter
1 8 oz semi-sweet chocolate
2¼ cups sugar
1 cup water
1 Tbsp instant coffee granules
9 eggs

Put in a greased bowl. Microwave 3 minutes. Whisk and microwave 3 minutes more.

Add 9 beaten eggs. Bake in springform pan at 250°F for an hour and 40 minutes.

Let it cool on the counter and then place it in the fridge for at least an hour (in the freezer for 15 minutes if you need to serve it sooner).

Devotion

There are some connections that are too perfectly timed to be coincidence. They are fingerprints of divine orchestration and evidence that God sees our future long before we do.

It's the kind of timing that follows us through seasons, cities, careers, heartbreaks, reinventions, and growth.

There are friends who show up not just for celebrations, but for course-corrections, prayers, pivots, and life's holy turning points. They are the iron that sharpens us. The wisdom that anchors us. The voice of reason God uses when ours gets shaky. God didn't just allow these friendships… He intended them.

One of the quiet graces of life is discovering that the people God binds to our spirits become living reminders that we are never walking our story alone. He always sends the ones we need, right on time.

Not by coincidence, but by covenant.

SCRIPTURE (NIV):
"When the time is right, the Lord will make it happen."
— Isaiah 49:8

PRAYER:
Lord, thank You for the provisions you send to us to remind us of Your perfect timing. Bless these covenant encounters and help me to steward them well. May my friendship to others and my service to You always reflect Your heart and follow Your Divine Will. Amen.

Amy's Spiced Tea

Tea:
4 family-size tea bags
1 frozen orange juice (regular size can)
3 OJ cans of water
24 oz pineapple juice
1 cup sugar

Spice:
2 cinnamon sticks
1 Tbsp cloves

Use a Dutch oven, and fill ⅓ of Dutch oven with water. Boil water and make strong tea, then remove tea bags. Add 1 frozen can of orange juice (regular size) and then 3 cans-full of water. Add pineapple juice and sugar.

Place sticks of cinnamon and cloves in a cheesecloth and tie off. Add to tea.

Leave the tea in the Dutch oven or put on low in a crockpot to serve.

"This spiced tea recipe is my momma's. I travel to Mississippi and go into the house and am welcomed by Momma and the wonderful taste and smell of this tea!!! It is love, comfort and home all rolled in one!!!"

—*Amy Burnett*

Amy Burnett

Another sweetheart of a friend that I met through Lauren is Amy Burnett. This girl. I tell you, when God poured out love, compassion, and thoughtfulness, Amy got a double dose. And on top of that, she could be a stand-up comedienne!

When we're together, we laugh until we cry. It was Lauren, Amy, CeCe and Lorrie in those early days in Nashville. We were single and lighting up Nashville. We loved Jesus, and we loved life. We all live in different towns now. But to this day we try to all get together at least once a year to spend a weekend in our pajamas, wear no makeup, cook, eat, and tell our "You can't make this stuff up" stories!

We even had T-shirts printed that say that. It's just so neat to have Christian girlfriends who will let you tell your stories, filled with mess-ups and mistakes, that often put you in a "not so positive light" and know that they won't judge you. But they also don't let you leave without praying for you and saying, "Tammi, God wants better for you. Now, get your head on straight, your heart in the right place and your eyes focused on the word of God!"

Amy is sharing her mama's spiced tea recipe (on previous page 111).

Devotion

The world offers surface-level connections, but God gives us people who become spiritual mirrors: those who remind us who we are, who we belong to, and who we are becoming in Christ.

What makes some friendships truly powerful is that they don't just comfort you, they correct in love. They pray you back into alignment when life knocks you off course. They cheer for your healing, not your hiding. They speak life, truth, and accountability wrapped in compassion.

These are the relationships that make room for honesty without shame, laughter without pretense, and growth without isolation. They celebrate joy and sit with sorrow. They hold your stories, not as ammunition, but as intercession. And when you forget who you are, they remind you whose you are.

The world teaches independence. The Kingdom teaches interdependence. We are not built to thrive alone. God designed us to walk in community where we build each other up in love.

SCRIPTURE (NIV):
"Therefore encourage one another and build each other up, just as in fact you are doing."
— 1 Thessalonians 5:11 (NIV)

PRAYER:
Lord, thank You for friendships rooted in both love and truth. Help me honor these relationships and grow into the kind of friend who prays, encourages, and speaks life into other's with grace. Amen.

Hummingbird Cake

Cake:
2¾ cups all-purpose flour, plus more for dusting
1 cup pecan pieces, toasted
3 ripe bananas, chopped
½ cup fresh pineapple, finely chopped
1 tsp ground cinnamon
1/2 tsp nutmeg, freshly grated
½ tsp ginger, ground
1 ¼ tsp baking soda
½ tsp salt
3 large eggs, room temperature
1¾ cups granulated sugar
1 cup vegetable oil

Frosting:
16 oz. cream cheese, room temperature
12 Tbsp unsalted butter, cubed, room temperature
2 cups confectioners' sugar
1 Tbsp lemon zest
1 tsp vanilla extract

Cake: First, put the pecans on a baking sheet and toast for about 7 minutes at 325°F. Remove from oven and let cool.

Then grease and flour two 8" round cake pans and line with parchment paper. You'll also want to grease and flour the parchment paper.

Combine the pecans with the bananas, pineapple and ½ cup flour in a small bowl.

In a separate bowl, whisk the remaining 2¼ cups flour, the cinnamon, nutmeg, ginger, baking soda and salt. Beat the eggs and granulated sugar with a mixer on high speed until thick and light, 5 minutes. Gradually add in the vegetable oil.

Sprinkle the flour mixture over the egg mixture, then gently fold to make a thick batter. Next, add in the pecan-fruit mixture. Transfer the batter to the prepared pans. Bake until the cakes are firm and a toothpick inserted into the middle comes out clean, 50 to 55 minutes. Cool in the pans on a rack, 25 minutes, then invert the cakes onto the rack to cool completely.

Frosting: Cream cheese needs to be room temperature. Beat the cream cheese in a large bowl with a mixer until smooth and creamy. Gradually beat in the butter until combined. Sift the confectioners' sugar over the cream cheese mixture and beat until smooth. Add the lemon zest and vanilla and beat until light and fluffy.

Place one cake layer on a serving plate. Spread about half of the frosting on top, then cover with the other cake layer. Spread the remaining frosting over the top and sides of the cake. You can add more toasted pecans to the top and sides of the cake!

Allen Lenard and Family

I'm not really sure where to begin with the Lenard family. But let me say, my life was forever changed when Allen Lenard reached out to me on Facebook and asked me to do one of my "Feed Your Soul" segments on "Lenard's Roadside Stand" just north of Monroe. You see, I had started this weekly segment on KNOE TV called "Feed Your Soul". It focused mainly on restaurants that used local farmers for their dishes. When I traveled to that vegetable and fruit pop-up, I discovered the story wasn't the roadside stand. It was Allen himself! He was a real-life hero. On this day when I stopped by the stand, Donna, Allen's mother, and her granddaughter Sadi were manning the stand. She proceeded to tell me that Allen was busy at the farm getting ready to go to the hurricane that was about to slam into south Louisiana. I said, excuse me, he's going to the hurricane. Most everyone in south Louisiana had been told to evacuate. I'll stop right here and let you know that if Allen is reading this, he's not happy with me. lol He never likes the spotlight to shine on him. He never wants the credit. So forgive me Allen! I just have to say that when most Louisiana men spend their free time hunting, fishing, or golfing (and nothing wrong with that, mind you) he spends his free time going to wherever there is a crisis.

He was getting ready on that hot summer day in July 2019 to meet Hurricane Barry head-on. It was about to make landfall. He would take his big four-wheel-drive truck, airboat and other equipment to help rescue those in nursing homes or stranded by high water. A one-man Cajun army. So on that day, my life changed when I met Allen, Donna, Sadi and Makin. I learned in a 20-minute interview with Allen that life's not about trying to make enough money to take luxury vacations and buy fancy cars, but it's about doing things every day with purpose and meaning. I fell in love with them all. The Lenard's taught me to put experiences before material possessions and to put others before yourself. Lenards, I love you.

Allen's favorite dessert of mine is Hummingbird cake (on previous page).

I asked Donna Hebert Lenard to share a treasured recipe for this book. Since she had operated a restaurant in Swartz, Louisiana, for several years, and the fact I'd eaten several meals at their house that she and Allen prepared, I said I trust whatever you send to me! She shared the Lenard's Chicken and Dressing recipe (see page 117).

Devotion

Some people preach the Gospel with words, but others preach it with their lives. They are the kind of servant-hearted souls who do not wait for a stage, a platform, applause, or recognition. They recognize the greatest acts of love usually happen far away from cameras or headlines. A life like this reminds us that the measure of a person is not found in comfort, but in sacrifice.

The world teaches us to chase success, but the Kingdom calls us to give ourselves away. Real greatness is almost never loud. It is the truck that drives toward disaster when everyone else is driving away. It is service without spotlight. It is compassion in motion. It is what Jesus meant when He said, "Follow Me."

Meeting people like this reorders your soul. They remind you that possessions fade, but purpose leaves a legacy. They don't live to be noticed, they live to be useful.

Some people store up comfort. Others, store up eternal deposits made every time they step into someone else's storm. Their life testifies that love is not just a feeling, but a response.

Jesus said the greatest among you will be a servant.

SCRIPTURE (NIV):
"Whoever wants to become great among you must be your servant, and whoever wants to be first must be your slave—just as the Son of Man did not come to be served, but to serve."
— Matthew 20:26–28

PRAYER:
Lord, thank You for the quiet heroes who live Your love in action. Bless those who serve without seeking recognition and let their example stir something holy in us. Teach me to value purpose over comfort and people over possessions. Help me live a life that reflects Your heart of compassion, sacrifice, and servant love. Amen.

Chicken and Dressing

1 hen boiled with salt and pepper
1 gallon of chicken broth
10" skillet of cornbread
3 large bell peppers
2 small bunches of green onions
1 medium stalk of celery
2 medium white onions
1 dozen eggs
Oil or butter

Debone the chicken and place one layer in the bottom of the baking dish. Sauté bell pepper, green onion celery and onion in vegetable oil, one stick of butter or the fat from the top of the boiled chicken broth.

Crumble cornbread in large pan. Add sauteed, cooked and cooled vegetables to cornbread and mix well. Add the raw eggs. Add broth and make sure all of cornbread is saturated. Add salt and pepper. Cook at 375°F until firm.

Tammi and Sadi

Lenard Family

Curtis Hilbun

Curtis Hilbun and I met for the first time backstage at the Grand Ole Opry in Nashville. Even though we grew up in neighboring parishes in Louisiana. He, in Franklin Parish. Me, in Madison Parish. He is a professional photographer and has taken photos of the some of the biggest stars in country music on their biggest stages. Dolly Parton loves this guy. She knows him by name. He's often asked to come photograph her at specific events. Those photos have graced the cover of national magazines for decades.

So when Curtis and I bumped into each other that night at the Opry all those years ago and he said, "You're Tammi Arender!" (and he said my last name correctly!) I knew we'd be friends for life. And we have been. We share such a bond from the way we were raised to the work we do. We can talk for hours on the phone about the frustrations (and joys) of covering the country music entertainment industry. He and I both often call each other when we're traveling to and from Tennessee to Louisiana or vice versa. We also share our love of good food! So, I was thrilled when Curtis said he'd submit his gumbo recipe!

Curtis' Tried and True Louisiana Gumbo (see recipe on page 120).

Okay, the secret to this gumbo is the roux. The roux is the flour/fat base that flavors and thickens the gumbo! If you burn it, you must start over! The secret to a good roux is to cook it slow and steady, at least for an hour until you get it to the darkness you desire. Some people like a caramel colored roux, some like a roux that is as dark as chocolate. It's a matter of your preference. But one thing is certain: when you cook the roux, you cannot be distracted! If you walk away for 45 seconds, it could burn. So... if you have small children, send them to grandma's house so you won't be distracted!

Devotion

We often know when God has placed someone in our path on purpose, but sometimes we don't. Sometimes we reject friendships that make us uncomfortable. God often uses friendships to give us perspective and help us see life from another angle. Many times, these are the people who understand the call, the cost, and the assignment, and show up to help us get back on track.

God can give you someone who knows your background and your journey forward, someone who shares your faith and your fire, someone who shows up not just for the highlight reel but for the hard days too.

We all face hardship. Days when we feel we can't drag ourselves out of bed. However, when we embrace friendships that can… for lack of better phrasing… kick our butts sometimes, we learn that we not only need that, we also can be that for others. We can stand in the gap and offer the tough love when it's needed.

SCRIPTURE (NIV):
"Two are better than one, because they have a good return for their labor… If either of them falls down, one can help the other up."
— Ecclesiastes 4:9–10

PRAYER:
Lord, thank You for the friends who walk beside us in those tough moments with both calling and companionship. Bless them for the gifts they use and the way they reflect Your corrections and renewing spirit. Help me to be the support for others that You call me to be, in whatever capacity You will. Amen.

Curtis' Tried and True Louisiana Gumbo

8 boneless chicken breasts, shredded
  (I cook mine in the Crock-Pot beforehand)
3 lb Tasso, cut into small pieces, fried and drained
3 lb Conecuh sausage, fried and drained
2 lb andouille sausage, fried and drained
9 boneless pork chops, cut into small pieces
2 lb Gulf shrimp, deveined
2 lb frozen okra
1 lb lump crab meat
2 white onions, finely chopped
6 stalks of celery, finely chopped
2 bell peppers, finely chopped
2 Tbsp garlic, minced
5 boxes chicken broth spices
3 Tbsp garlic powder
3 Tbsp onion powder
¼ cup of Worcestershire sauce
Hot sauce to taste
5 bay leaves

After the roux has cooked until the desired color, add chopped vegetables to the roux. When you first add the vegetables to the hot roux, there will be a lot of steam! Don't get burned! Once you add the vegetables, the mix will tighten up. This is normal. Continue stirring until veggies are tender.

Add chicken broth to the roux/vegetable mixture and stir well. Reduce heat and allow the broth to combine with the roux and cook for about ten minutes.

Add chicken, Tasso, sausage, and pork chops.

Add bay leaves, Worcestershire sauce, and a few dashes of hot sauce (if desired). Cover and cook for approximately 90 minutes. Additional chicken broth may be required.

Add frozen okra, crabmeat, and shrimp at the end of cooking. Cook for approximately 30 minutes.

Enjoy over a scoop of rice topped with fresh gumbo filé.

Myra Gatling-Akers

My friend Myra. Love her. She and I met in the singles group at First Baptist Church in West Monroe, Louisiana, many moons ago. We were on fire for Jesus, but we also were single and were setting the dating world on fire. Myra, Esther, Kathy and Marilyn. Our little singles group was a force to be reckoned with! I look back on our time together, and it brings a tear to my eye. There's a bond between us that's almost indescribable.

Back to Myra. She is a blonde bombshell. Even my nephew, Cameron, when he was young, saw her for the first time and exclaimed, "It's Barbie! Real-life Barbie!" Myra is that beautiful. Inside and out! I've got several "almost unbelievable" stories involving our single escapades, but I'll share this one. I will change the names to protect the innocent.

I was in love, maybe even obsessed, with Tom (not his real name, but it did start with a T.) Tom was from Rayville, 20 miles east of Monroe. I was living in Monroe at the time. It was a Friday night, and I fully expected to see Tom when I got off work. But instead, he said he was tired and just going home to Rayville for the night. My woman's intuition kicked in. I knew this man wasn't going home. So, I called Myra and said, "Get your stakeout clothes on." We're headed to downtown Monroe and stake out Tom's favorite bar/hangout. Just like in the movies, we sat in my car across the street from said hangout for hours. Myra didn't complain once that I was preventing her from getting precious time with her boyfriend as well as costing her sleep! And sure enough, around 1:00a.m. Tom comes walking out of the bar holding the hand of a cute blonde with curly hair. I jumped out of the car and chased them down the sidewalk. Yes, I certainly did! Because I didn't want Tom to be able to "deny" that he was with this person. I wanted him to know he got caught! So I screamed, "Tom!" He and his "friend" turned around, with eyes as big as saucers, knowing he'd been busted. Honestly, I don't even know what I said, other than, "Caught you!" I didn't cause a scene. I just turned around and ran back to the car, crying my eyes out. Myra was there. Holding my hand and reminding me that Tom wasn't worth my tears. Crazy sidebar to that story? The woman Tom with, Lisa Boullt, actually lived in Nashville and would end up becoming a dear friend! She had moved from northeast Louisiana to Music City to work in the music industry. She worked many years for the legendary Charlie Daniels.

Lisa called me the next day and explained that she and Tom were just friends. She begged me to believe her. She asked me to lunch when I relocated to Nashville. She is a doll and a peach. I'm forever grateful I got to meet her. I just hate it was under those circumstances.

But back to Myra. That was just one example of how she was there for me. Always and forever one of my dearest friends.

Myra loved my flourless ginger chocolate muffins. One of the only healthy things I make!

Devotion

Anyone can celebrate with you when life is tidy, but the friends God assigns to you are the ones who sit beside you in the car while your heart is breaking, mascara running, and dignity somewhere under the floorboard… and they stay anyway.

Not someone who always has to fix the wound, but someone who refuses to let you bleed alone.

Jesus meets us before He corrects us. He comforts us before He redirects us. He stands with us in heartbreak long before He calls us back to healing.

Look at the beauty God wove from the ashes of your heartbreaks. God is a Redeemer not just of mistakes, but of tragedy. He knew long before you did that one day you would see a blessing from your toil. Nothing about that is coincidence, which is a providence of His word.

This story is a reminder that God does not waste our detours. He folds even heartbreak into purpose and brings us good from all things. Sometimes the very moment we thought was humiliation turns into the doorway to our healing and strengthening of our faith.

SCRIPTURE (NIV):
"And we know that all things work together for good to them that love God, to them who are the called according to his purpose"
— Romans 8:28

PRAYER:
Lord, thank You for the blessings You have given me. Thank you for gently reminding me of my worth when my confidence is shaken. Thank you for the ones who sit with me in the mess, pray me through the pain, and point me back to You. Help me be that person to others and love them with the same loyalty and grace I've been given. Amen.

Flourless Ginger Chocolate Muffins

3 ripe bananas
1 cup creamy peanut butter (or almond butter)
2 large eggs
1 tsp vanilla
¼ cup honey, molasses or maple syrup
¼ cup sugar or artificial sweetener
¼ cup cocoa powder
1 tsp baking soda
¼ cup dark chocolate chips (optional)

Start by mashing the bananas in a food processor. Then, add the peanut butter, eggs, vanilla, and honey into the bowl. Pulse until they are well combined.

Next, add the cocoa powder and baking soda. Mix again until combined.

Add the dark chocolate chips with a spoon. Do not pulse.

Bake in a preheated oven at 350°F for 18 to 20 minutes or until the toothpick comes out clean.

Lisa Boullt

I've briefly mentioned my friend Lisa Boullt. (Refer back to the Myra Gatling-Akers story and you'll discover how I met Lisa.) Brief recap, I thought she was cheating with my boyfriend at the time, and I chased her and him down a sidewalk outside a bar one late night in Monroe! The things we do in the name of love (and jealousy!).

But the bond that formed under those unusual circumstances has been unbreakable. Lisa is one of the kindest, sweetest, most thoughtful people I know. So I knew I had to ask her to contribute a recipe. Plus, you need to hear her story. How she's giving back, changing lives and honoring her late sister Andrea. I encourage you to read her book, "17 Again." Lisa is an incredible author and songwriter.

Lisa decided to offer up her chicken spaghetti recipe along with the story behind it. Thank you, Lisa! Love you big!

From Lisa: "I chose this recipe for a few reasons. Mike's (Lisa's boyfriend) mom, Carla, used to make it for us, and she gave me the recipe before she passed, so it became a favorite in our home. When I was writing my book, "17 Again" about my sister Andrea, who passed away in 1993, I remembered a story that Libbie Harrison from LOPA, Louisiana Organ Procurement Association, had shared with me in 2021. Her son, Justin, passed away in August 1997, and he became an organ donor. Libbie had the chance to meet Marilyn, who received Justin's heart. Before her transplant, Marilyn never liked chicken spaghetti but after her heart transplant, that was the first thing she craved. This was such a special story that needed to be shared, so I asked Libbie's permission to use it in my book. Libbie started working at LOPA full time in 2000 and continues to love on families going through what she did. Every time I make it, I think of Carla and Justin."

Devotion

The fact that one of the most meaningful connections in your life were born out of a moment of heartbreak says everything about how God works: He takes what could have remained a wound and turns it into a witness. Only God can turn accusation into affection, suspicion into sisterhood, and a confrontation into a lifelong connection.

God reminds us that deep compassion from others is often born from their own deep pain. He sends people who have walked through valleys and can testify to the hope we have in God.

We learn that the beauty of a surrendered heart stops asking "Why me?" and starts asking "Lord, use me."

Some friends reflect our past, but others help us move into our purpose. A reminder that God's plan for us is always deeper than anything we go through.

SCRIPTURE (NIV):

"For I know the plans I have for you," declares the LORD, "plans to prosper you and not to harm you, plans to give you hope and a future." — Jeremiah 29:11

PRAYER:

Lord, thank You for turning sorrow into purpose. Thank You for giving me hope born out of Your redeeming hand. Teach me to look for the blessings in all things and share that testimony with others through Your love and compassion. Use my story to continue bringing hope and healing wherever it is needed. Amen.

Lisa's Chicken Spaghetti

4 boneless chicken breasts, cooked and shredded
1 can cream of mushroom soup
1 can of chicken broth
1 can Rotel tomatoes with green chilis
1 small jar pimentos
16 oz Velveeta shreds
12 oz spaghetti or linguine noodles
Salt and pepper to taste

Boil pasta until done. Mix together soup, broth, tomatoes and pimentos.

Layer in a baking dish: Pasta, chicken, soup mixture and cover with cheese. Bake at 350°F until the cheese is melted. Stir mixture before serving and add salt and pepper to taste.

For added flavor, I like to top it with Louisiana Hot Sauce.

Spicy Crawfish Spaghetti

1 lb crawfish tails
1 can mild Rotel tomatoes
1 cup onion, chopped
1 can cream of shrimp soup
½ cup bell pepper, chopped
12 oz package thin spaghetti
¾ cup celery, chopped
3 cups water
1 Tbsp paprika
Salt and pepper to taste
1 tsp Louisiana hot sauce
Oil

Sauté onions, bell pepper and celery in oil until onions are clear.

Add tomatoes, seasonings, soup and water. Bring to a boil, add spaghetti, and cook for 20 minutes on medium heat.

Add crawfish tails and cook for an additional 10 minutes or until spaghetti is done.

Terri Howell

When I was first starting out as a reporter and anchor in Louisiana, I had to cover a lot of politics. If you're not familiar with the Louisiana political scene, just Google it. It's a sport. There is quite a cast of characters who have either ended up as the subject of a movie or in jail! Don't get me wrong, we've also had lots of politicians who've done a lot of good and acted with integrity.

When Buddy Roemer was running for governor in 1987, he had a scheduler named Terri Howell. We hit it off. It's like we were instant friends. So when I moved to Baton Rouge, which is where she was located, our friendship blossomed. This woman and I have some stories to tell! We both had extraordinary family drama over the years. (We've all had family drama, right? We all know you can choose your friends; you can't choose your family!) But suffice it to say, she and I helped each other out by either being on a "stakeout" to find out what some of these kinfolks were up to or just listened to each for hours on end about some of the poor choices those around us made.

Terri started working for Carnival Cruise Line. She's always been in the travel business. And to this day, if anyone with the last name Arender tries to get on a Carnival Cruise ship, there's a red flag because of an "incident" with one of my family members. Not making this up! I'll spare you the details, but poor Terri had to suffer through some unbearable things because of this incident. But she was gracious enough to separate me, and our friendship, from the actions of those near to me. Love you, girl!

Terri has offered up two recipes. Her Cajun crab cakes and spicy crawfish spaghetti.

Devotion

Everyone has some degree of family drama, but not everyone has someone willing to walk alongside them through it without judgment. That is a Christlike quality, because Jesus does the same for us. He sees beyond the mess and calls us by our identity, not by our associations or past.

A grace-filled life reflects Your character when life tries to drag your name through the mud. They treat your name as separate from the hurt of the world.

Your love reminds us that love is not blind, but it sees clearly and chooses to love us, anyway. In a world where people are quick to distance themselves at the first sign of inconvenience or trouble, You remain a gift to us.

God sees you in the purity of your heart more than the pollution of the situation around you. Let nothing separate you from that love.

SCRIPTURE (NIV):
"Neither height nor depth, nor anything else in all creation, will be able to separate us from the love of God that is in Christ Jesus our Lord."
— Romans 8:39

PRAYER:
Lord, thank You for loving me through the messiness of life. That no embarrassment, complication, or misunderstanding can separate me from You. Heal me of my wound and transform my life to reflect more of Your love. Teach me to offer the same covering, compassion, and faithfulness to others that You have for me. Amen.

Cajun Crabcakes

1½ lb lump crab meat
1½ tsp Worcestershire sauce
3 green onions, finely chopped
¼ tsp salt
¼ cup parsley, minced
½ tsp Louisiana hot sauce
3 Tbsp yogurt
1 cup plain dry bread crumbs
3 Tbsp fresh lemon juice
3 large eggs (egg whites only)
2 cloves garlic, minced
4 Tbsp vegetable oil
1½ tsp dry mustard

Mix all ingredients in a bowl. Form into patties. Fry in a skillet in oil until golden brown on both sides.

Nancy's Meatballs

1 lb ground beef
1 egg
1 Tbsp Worcestershire sauce
¾ cup Parmesan cheese (shredded)
2 Tbsp ketchup (or BBQ sauce)
¼ cup sour cream (this is my addition)
½ cup breadcrumbs (I use Italian breadcrumbs)
1 onion (chopped)
Salt and pepper to taste

Combine ingredients and roll into whatever size meatballs you desire. Brown in skillet or in oven at 350°F degrees until brown. I prefer cooking on top of the stove so I can use the flavoring from the meat in my sauce.

You can use whatever sauce you prefer to prepare your dish. I use Raos Marinara because I found it was just as good as when I used to make tomato sauce from scratch, and it saves time. And I add a little sugar to the sauce to cut the acidity. (To taste)

* When making the meatballs, you can use another egg and/or more bread crumbs if you want them to hold well together or follow the recipe allowing the meat to break apart a little and have some meat sauce as well as meatballs.

"My uncle specialized in two things, and we all loved going to his house whenever he cooked anything. It was either crawfish bisque or spaghetti and meatballs. I had him give me his secret to making spaghetti and meatballs. Uncle Bobby also had the best crawfish boils! I miss Louisiana sometimes! But I really love Coronado, California"

—Nancy Nelson Howden

Nancy Nelson Howden

My Nancy. I'll never forget the day I visited Bethany Church in Baton Rouge. I sat right behind Nancy Nelson. She was a fan of TuneIn, the WBRZ morning show I was co-hosting with Leo Honeycutt. When she turned around to shake my hand during the "say hello to your neighbor portion of the church service, she looked at me and said, "We're going to be friends!" She was right. We became friends and shortly thereafter became roommates.

God broke the mold when He made this woman. I loved her from the get-go. She listened to me for hours on end talk about my "boy" problems. And when Don Ragusa broke my heart, she honestly kept me from jumping off the I-10 bridge. I was devastated beyond description. If it weren't for Nancy and the Holy Bible, I don't know that I would have survived that heartbreak.

Nancy lived with me while she was going to nursing school. I'll never forget when she graduated, she said she was going to San Diego, California for just six months as a "traveling nurse," and then she'd be back to Baton Rouge. But, she met Rick. Nancy never returned to Baton Rouge except for occasional visits. She'd found her forever love and forever home in California. So, I started making yearly treks to San Diego to visit her. Because I had to have my "Nancy fix."

We even decided that I should try to get a job in San Diego and be close to her. So, on my next trip I took my box of resume tapes (VHS tapes of my TV news work because this was before YouTube existed!). I got a news director at a San Diego TV station to take notice. He even offered me a reporting job. I remember calling my daddy and telling him. I was so excited. This was a major market and, other than Nashville or Dallas, the only TV market I wanted to work in. When I told Daddy that I had been offered a job there, there was silence on the other end. After several long seconds, he said, "That's too far.". But I argued that we would plan trips and we could fly to see each other every other month. I was already living in Nashville and struggled to get home every few months, since it was a nearly 8 hour drive. I was a daddy's girl. I went to great lengths never to disappoint him. So even with this big job offer in a major market, I couldn't disappoint Billy Ray Arender. I turned it down and stayed in Nashville. To this day, I've always wondered what life would have been like if I'd taken the job in San Diego and been close to "my Nancy." But everything happens for a reason. No regrets, right?

I am so happy Nancy wanted to share a recipe. She's a great cook and we've enjoyed many conversations and great meals in her kitchen.

Devotion

There are relationships that save your life in ways the world will never see. Not through grand gestures, but through late-night listening, truth spoken with tenderness, and the kind of compassion that refuses to leave when heartbreak hits hard. They stand guard over your heart at a time when it is breaking wide open. That is ministry.

Then there are the choices we make because of love.. Sometimes obedience doesn't look glamorous. Sometimes it looks like staying and sometimes it looks like going. Faithfulness means letting go of a dream in order to honor a relationship God entrusted to you and His purpose over your life.

Not all "what ifs" are regrets. Some are simply reminders that love guided the road we chose, and God stayed in the middle of it the whole way. Some of those reminders come through people who encourage us and stand with us.

SCRIPTURE (NIV):
"I thank my God every time I remember you." — Philippians 1:3

PRAYER;
Lord, thank You for the ones who carry our hearts through the hardest seasons and remind us we are not alone, but guided through Your purpose and protection. Bless those who provide us that shelter. Help me honor You by trusting that every path, even the ones I didn't take, is covered by Your hand.
Amen.

Slow Cooker Chicken Tortilla Soup

2 cups chicken, shredded or cubed
10-oz can enchilada sauce
1 medium onion, chopped
1 can black beans
1 can corn
1 box chicken broth (I use low sodium)
½ package taco seasoning
1 Tbsp Tony Chachere's seasoning
1 bay leaf
1 Tbsp cilantro, chopped
1 lime
shredded cheddar cheese
7 corn tortillas for homemade tortilla strips
Vegetable oil

Place chicken, black beans, corn, enchilada sauce, and onion in slow cooker. Pour in chicken broth until it reaches near the top of the pot. Add Taco seasoning, Tony Chachere's seasoning, cilantro and bay leaf. Squeeze in lime juice for extra flavor. Cover, and cook on low setting for 6 to 8 hours, or high setting for 3 to 4 hours.

Preheat oven to 400°F.

Lightly brush both sides of tortillas with oil and add taco or Tony's seasoning. Cut tortillas into strips, then spread on a baking sheet.

Bake in preheated oven until crisp, about 10 to 15 minutes.

Sprinkle shredded cheddar cheese and tortilla strips over soup for an attractive and appealing presentation. Makes 8 medium-sized bowl servings.

Janie West

My friend Janie is such a special person. She is one of the first people I met after moving to Nashville. I remember my tiny little apartment downtown on the Cumberland River. It was basically a closet with a bathroom! But that was okay because I literally had nothing but a mattress on the floor, an answering machine—yep, this was long before cell phones and voicemail!, and a coffee pot. That was it! Since I lived downtown, I wanted to find a church close by. First Baptist Church on Broadway was my church home in Nashville from day one. On the first day I attended, I met Pastor Frank Lewis, a dear friend to this day, and Janie West. I found out she was also a Louisiana girl! She is originally from New Orleans, Louisiana. We knew we'd be buddies because of our Bayou State connection. To this day, she's that friend that we can go months without talking, but pick up where we left off in the blink of an eye. We've talked for hours about relationships, the music business and the mysterious ways in which God works. She's been a prayer partner and prayer warrior all these years. Nashville wouldn't be the same without Janie and neither would I!

She shared her tortilla soup recipe (see previous page).

Devotion

Prayer partners are a treasure. They are the people who hear you in your need, and carry it to the throne of God. When someone prays with you and for you, they become part of your spiritual foundation. Their faith helps hold you steady when your own feels thin.

The sweetest part of friendships like this is that they are not weakened by silence. Months may pass, life may get busy, seasons may shift — but the bond is built on the Spirit, not on constant communication. The heart recognizes what God knit together, and distance can't unravel it.

Janie is a reminder that God is thoughtful with placement. He knew you would need a familiar heart in a new season, a voice of prayer in a city of ambition, and a sister who would remind you of who you are when life tries to blur the edges. Nashville may have been the location — but she was part of the provision.

These are the friendships that make you better, stronger, more grounded, and more prayerful because they keep pointing you back to Jesus.

SCRIPTURE (NIV):
"as you help us by your prayers. Then many will give thanks on our behalf for the gracious favor granted us in answer to the prayers of many."
— 2 Corinthians 1:11

PRAYER:
Lord, thank You for friends who pray us through seasons of growth, uncertainty, and change. Bless them for being a steady voice of faith and a reflection of Your care. Help me to cherish serving others in the same way to strengthen other people's spirits and remind them they never walk alone. Amen.

The Empty Plate:
Rest Is the Missing Ingredient in a Busy Home

Our lives are full of motion. The kitchen hums, laundry turns, to-do lists grow, and dinner somehow appears like clockwork. From sunrise to bedtime, you're meeting needs, fixing problems, and keeping life stitched together for everyone else. Somewhere in the mix, though, it's easy to forget one person: yourself.

Many of us live with an empty plate. You feed others first, often forgetting to sit down and savor the meal. You pour yourself into the doing for others and forget that rest is not a luxury; it's a necessity. It's the ingredient that brings everything else together.

It's easy to spot needs in others, such as a tired spouse, a child needing attention, an elderly parent who needs a hand. Yet, our caregiver's needs often hide behind a smile. Still, it shows up as irritability, fatigue, or that quiet ache that whispers, "something's missing."

Constant giving without rest leads to depletion. Just as food nourishes the body, small things that I talk about in *Cup of Comfort* (see pages 94-95) such as walking at sunset or creating something, can fill our cup, but it is the stillness in rest that nourishes the soul.

Knowing that rest isn't a reward at the end of the list, but a key ingredient in the recipe that keeps you able to love, serve, and care with joy. Even God, after creating the world, rested, not because He was tired, but to model the sacred rhythm of work and renewal.

Remember that doing small things you like fills your cup, but resting…true rest…fills your plate.

And that's the meat of it.

Simple Ways to Fill Your Plate Again

Claim a Quiet Moment.
Before anyone else wakes, or after the
house settles, grab a cup of tea, coffee, or
warm lemon water and take ten minutes
for silence. Breathe. Stretch. Pray. Let your
thoughts untangle.

Say No Sometimes.
Saying no to one extra task can be saying
yes to your own peace. Protect your energy
the way you protect others' comfort.

Sit and Eat Slowly.
Take the time to choose one meal a
day to actually sit for. No rushing, no
multitasking. Just you, your food, and
gratitude for the moment.

Find Your Daily Rituals.
Maybe it's reading a book, or tending a
houseplant (see *Cup of Comfort* on pages
94-94). Do something daily that quiets the
noise and fills your heart.

Shellie Rushing Tomlinson

If there was anyone who could change the temperature of a room just by walking in, it's Shellie Rushing Tomlinson! There is no other person who can light a fire under you for Jesus than Shellie. All while making you laugh so hard you'll split your britches. Shellie and her sisters went to my high school, Tallulah Academy, for a few years. We played basketball and tennis together. Being a small school, we were all pretty close. But it wasn't until our adult years that the connection to Shellie grew stronger.

She married a farmer in East Carroll Parish. She'll tell you that there's nothing she takes more seriously than being her beloved farmer's bride (other than being a Jesus follower!). But she knew she had a calling on her life to share that love for Jesus. And in a unique way. She's a gifted author and speaker. That girl is some kind of funny.

Her schedule is absolutely chaotic but yet she still finds time to check on me and, more importantly, pray for me. It's not unusual for me to get a text or a call from her out of the blue and she'll say God has put you on my heart. Tell me what's going on? She even drove 8 hours one way to watch me say two paragraphs on the Grand Ole Opry stage! Little backstory here. The Grand Ole Opry is the most iconic stage in the country music world. The likes of Dolly Parton, Loretta Lynn, Garth Brooks, Reba McEntire and countless other legendary country singers have performed on that stage. Well, I'm a huge country music fan so that stage is hallowed ground. Since I can't carry a tune in a bucket (just ask anyone who sits next to me at church!), I knew I'd never get to "perform" on that stage. But I did get invited to "speak" on that storied stage. It was part of the Veterans Day Concert put on by the Medical Music Group in 2022. Several speakers would recite some lines while an orchestra played patriotic songs. I happened to mention this to Shellie during one of our calls and she drove all the way from Lake Providence, Louisiana to Nashville to be there! She even came a

day early to follow me around on a video shoot for one of my Rural Road Trippin stories for RFD-TV. We had a ball. Laughed, talked, cried, and laughed some more. That girl is the real deal. Shellie has several inspirational books that are must-reads. Thank you, Shellie, for being that friend. And oh, by the way, one of her many incredible books is one called "Hungry is a Mighty Fine Sauce." Check it out!

Shellie's contribution is her garlic cheese grits.

Devotion

There are encouragers who tell you nice things, and there are encouragers who stir your spirit. The difference is anointing. They ignite you. They don't just cheer for you, they push you forward into boldness, the way a flame lights another wick without losing its own fire.

That is what Scripture means when it says to "bear one another's burdens." It is showing up when the support is felt, not just seen.

This is the beautiful mystery of God-ordained friendships: sometimes He uses another person's faith to revive our own. When they senses a tug from the Holy Spirit to pray, text, or call, they obey. Their obedience always bears fruit. Some of us water seeds. Some of us pull weeds. But encouragers are the sunshine, bringing the warmth that keeps you growing when you might otherwise wilt.

A friend like that reminds you that God still sees you. Still fights for you. Still sends reinforcements when your spirit feels thin. In those moments, you realize that encouragement is not a personality trait, but a mission for all of us from the Almighty.

SCRIPTURE (NIV):
"Bear one another's burdens, and thereby fulfill the law of Christ."
— Galatians 6:2 (NIV)

PRAYER:
Lord, thank You for the people whose joy and obedience breathe life into weary hearts. Bless them for carrying Your light and faithfully and pouring it into others. Help me become more reliable, present and the kind of encourager who doesn't just speak comfort, but stirs faith, but who shows up, lifts up, and points others back to You with bold and joyful love. Amen.

The Belle's Garlic Cheese Grits

8 cups water
2 cups quick-cooking grits
2 eggs
2 cups extra sharp cheddar cheese
½ lb Velvetta
1 stick butter
1 tsp of garlic
½ tsp cayenne pepper
  (use chili powder if you don't
  want them too spicy)
Salt and black pepper

Begin by taking a big glass bowl and combining two cups of quick cooking grits with 8 cups of water. (For the love… please don't use instant grits. Instant grits are not grits, and I'm going to leave that right there before I get all worked up).

Cook in the microwave on high for about 8 minutes. Afterwards, stir in a stick of butter, ½ pound of Velvetta, and one cup of grated sharp cheddar cheese. Now, we'll add two eggs, but we'll need to temper them first by cracking them into a separate small bowl and gradually stirring in a little of the hot grits. This prevents the eggs from cooking, y'all. You don't want scrambled eggs in your grits. Alongside your grits, that's okay, in your grits, that's not good and your mama's going to frown at you if she sees it. Once your eggs are tempered, we'll add 'em into the rest of our grits.

Now season 'em with a teaspoon of garlic powder and a ½ teaspoon of cayenne pepper. Salt and pepper, to taste and finish with the remaining cup of grated sharp cheddar. IF these are for us, I'm going to add diced jalapenos. If I'm serving them to a crowd, like the baby shower, I'm going to leave them out. Slide in a 375 degree oven and cook for about 30 minutes until they're hot through and through, beginning to firm up, and the cheese on top has melted. YUM! That's the Belle's Baked Cheese Grits and they're mighty good eating, from the All Things Southern kitchen to yours!

Geaux Nuts

¼ cup maple syrup
½ cup butter
2 cups walnuts
2 cups pecans
2 cups cashews
¼ cup sugar
1 tsp chili powder
1 tsp salt
¼ tsp cinnamon

Start by melting the butter and maple syrup together. Combine the sugar, chili powder, cinnamon and salt. Mix altogether in a big bowl until all nuts are covered. Pour them onto a greased cookie sheet covered with tinfoil. Bake at 325°F degrees for 25 minutes. Once out of the oven, stir the nuts around on the pan to make sure all are covered with this melted goodness. Let cool. I eat them a snack, put them in salads, over ice cream and in my cereal. So good!

David Miller

You know, they say men and women can't be just friends. Either one or the other wants something more. Something romantic.

And I have to admit, when I first met David Miller in Nashville, I did want something more. For a hot minute, I thought maybe he was the reason I moved to Nashville! That he would be the man who would have me picking out a church and a china pattern. But I quickly learned that David did not have "romantic" feelings for me. I would forever be in the friend zone.

At first, my feelings were hurt. But I soon realized what a true treasure it is to have a dedicated Christian friend who is closer than a brother.

So for the next 3 decades (and still counting), David and I would form a bond that I've had with no one other man. We are prayer partners, praise singers, tenant/landlord, activities partners, and exercise buddies. If there was ever anyone with whom I could be myself with, without fear of any judgment of any kind, it's David. I can be around him with no makeup, cancel at the last minute, tell him he's being a cheapskate (there is no more frugal man on the face of the planet!) and sing to the top of my lungs off key and he's still right there beside me. Talk about true-blue friendship.

I've truly been blessed to have this encourager, believer, prayer warrior, and friend in my life. Forever thankful that God allowed us to meet all those years ago when we were volunteering and leading worship at a Christmas party at the Nashville Rescue Mission (homeless shelter). Thank you, David, for being you.

David is not a cook and scoffed when I asked for a recipe. But one of his favorite things that I make is actually a snack. It's my "Geaux Nuts" recipe. So this is for you, David!

Devotion

The world loves to tell us that men and women can't be "just friends," but the Kingdom tells a different story. God does sometimes knit hearts together not for romance, but for spiritual companionship. A friendship that reflects a sibling's love, protection, prayer, and loyalty without needing anything more. When God assigns a brother or sister in Christ to your life, it is a rare and holy blessing.

We all likely have a story that proves that sometimes what we thought we wanted is not nearly as valuable as what God knew we needed. You hoped first for a love story, but what you received was a lifelong covering. Someone who has prayed you through storms, walked alongside you through seasons, and stayed steady through the years.

There is a deep gift in having a friend who expects nothing from you except authenticity. A person who makes room for your unfiltered thoughts, your off-key singing, your bad hair days, and your "please pray for me right now" moments, without having to share a romatic relationship.

This kind of friendship teaches us something about the Father's heart: that love without agenda is possible, and that being chosen as a friend is sometimes a greater honor than being pursued as a bride.

A witness in your life that God truly does surround us with His goodness through people.

SCRIPTURE (NIV):
"A man that hath friends must show himself friendly, and there is a friend that sticketh closer than a brother."
— Proverbs 18:24

PRAYER:
Lord, thank You for friendships that reflect Your purity, steadiness, and spiritual groundedness. Teach me to cherish these rare gifts and to honor the people who walk beside me in truth and love. May you show me how I can be as faithful a friend to others as they has been to me. Amen.

April Oed Hamilton

This is such an incredible story. I've mentioned that I moved to Charleston, West Virginia, to work at WOWK TV. This was in 2014 at the behest of my mentor, friend and former General Manager at WKRN in Nashville, Mike Sechrist. Charleston was a beautiful area with its mountains and rivers. The problem for me was it was too cold (I once stared at -9 below zero in the face for several days, and for this deep south girl, that was unacceptable!) and it was way too far from home. I went into a deep depression shortly after I took the job. I loved Mike and working for him, but I felt like a fish out of water. One bright spot was, Mike allowed me to do a weekly cooking segment for the TV station. I was thrilled. But quickly learned that I did not have countless recipes in my repertoire that I could cook from memory and look good on camera doing it! I decided to invite local chefs to come join me. April Hamilton was doing a weekly food column for the Charleston newspaper. And she liked to cook healthy. Something not in my wheelhouse! So, I invited her to join me on one of my weekly segments. Then she invited me to come do a cooking demonstration at the Charleston Farmer's Market. She and I quickly bonded. Food will do that, you know! But it was more than a love of food and cooking. This woman is a force. A force for good in the world. Everything she does, she does with passion. But shortly after connecting with her, I told her that as soon as Mike, the GM at WOWK, found my replacement on the anchor desk, he was going to let me out of my contract. He knew I was miserable, and he was kind enough to let me out of my contract way before it was up so I could go back home. When I told April that I would be returning to Louisiana because this outdoors girl couldn't take the winters in WV, she begged me to stay. She said you'll love WV in the summer and Fall. We can go whitewater rafting. We can go hiking. We can do all sorts of things in the great outdoors. Just you wait and see. Plus, we have fun in the kitchen! But I assured her that I would not be staying and would soon be back in Bayou Country as soon as Mike found my replacement. Six months later my cousin Lori showed up yet again with the U-Haul truck, helped pack me up, and I was back home in God's country. Then lo and behold, not a few months later, April calls me and said you're not going to believe this, but my husband has been transferred to Baton Rouge, Louisiana!! I said girl, you're going to think you've died and gone to heaven. Louisiana is a foodie's paradise. April quickly adapted to the Cajun culture. She is writing food columns for the Advocate and 225 Magazine. She has her own cookbook called Counter Intelligence. And now she's become a full-time nurse. And the story behind that is amazing. Do yourself a favor and Google April Oed Hamilton. Read her story. Get to know her and her daughter's story and you will be inspired. I may have only spent ten minutes in West Virginia but it was long enough to meet my new forever friend, April Oed Hamilton!

The recipe she's sharing with us is her personal peach pies!

Devotion

Some people cross our paths only because God refused to let distance keep us from meeting them. You may have a friend like mine where your time with them was brief, almost like a detour, but heaven knew it was an appointment. Sometimes the Lord will move us somewhere unfamiliar not because the place will change us, but because the person we need to meet is waiting there.

So often we think God is at work in the long seasons, such as years, decades, or the big chapters. But sometimes, His greatest gifts are placed inside temporary seasons, so that later, when life shifts again, the friendship continues on as if it had always belonged.

God never wastes discomfort. Your unhappiness does not cancel the purpose, and it can often highlight it. Even when you feel out of place, you are not out of God's will.

It always isn't the big "season" that produces the gifts; that is why obedience matters. Because when you go where God leads, even for "ten minutes," He places eternal friendships in your path that you might never have found otherwise.

SCRIPTURE (NIV):
"The Lord directs the steps of the righteous; He delights in every detail of their lives." — Psalm 37:23

PRAYER:
Lord, thank You for the connections You weave into our lives on purpose, even in place that feel temporary or uncomfortable. Help me always recognize the divine appointments You place along my path, and remind me that You never waste a single step for me. Amen.

April's Personal Peach Pies

5 medium peaches, unpeeled and thinly sliced
(about 3 cups)
½ cup light brown sugar, packed
2 Tbsp cornstarch
2 tsp fresh lemon juice
(from 1 small lemon)
½ tsp ground cinnamon
¼ tsp ground cardamom
¼ tsp kosher salt
Baking spray with flour
14.1 oz. package refrigerated pie dough
All-purpose flour
(for work surface)
1 large egg
1 Tbsp water
2 tsp granulated sugar

Preheat oven to 375°F.

Toss together peaches, brown sugar, cornstarch, lemon juice, cinnamon, cardamom, and salt in a medium bowl until fully coated. Set aside. Place 1 piecrust on a lightly floured work surface, and roll into a 13-inch round. I use a large round cookie cutter to cut dough into 3 (6-inch) rounds.

Spoon about ¼ cup peach mixture onto each circle. Fold dough edges up and over filling. (Dough will only partially cover filling). Whisk together egg and water in a small bowl. Lightly brush dough with egg mixture, and sprinkle evenly with granulated sugar.

Bake in preheated 375°F oven until crust is golden-brown and sugar has caramelized, 30 to 35 minutes. Remove from oven, and let cool on a wire rack for 15 minutes.

Micky's Hambone Soup

1 hambone
2 qt water
2 cups onion, diced
2 cups celery, diced
2 cups carrots, diced
1 ½ pounds dried navy beans
2 bay leaves
2 cloves garlic
1 tsp thyme
Salt and pepper to taste

Cooktop Option:

Soak beans overnight. Drain and set aside.

Place water and hambone in large pot with spices. Simmer 1 to 1.5 hours until meat falls off bone. Remove hambone from pot.

Add beans and simmer until they begin to turn soft. Remove bay leaves

Cut ham from bone and drop meat into pot. Add vegetables and simmer up to 2 hours. Salt and pepper to taste, serve.

Pressure Cooker Option:

Place dried beans and other ingredients in pressure cooker. Use the beans/chili setting for 50 minutes. Let pressure naturally release for 30 minutes.

Remove hambone and bay leaves. Shred meat as necessary.

Cook on slow another 2 hours. Salt and pepper to taste, serve.

Micky has made this recipe for his family for years. It was one of the first soups he prepared for Pam in 2022 when they began to see each other. Now married since 2023, Pam and Micky often share duties in the kitchen. When preparing this recipe, no one cuts vegetables more precisely than Micky, so that will always be his job.

Pam Bentley

I honestly could not let this book go to print without a submission from Pam Beatty Case Bentley. I use all of her names because I know her by all of them! This is another one of those stories where God had a purpose when He allowed her to cross my path. When I first started working at RFD-TV, the agriculture network in Nashville, I met Pam. I knew OF Pam before that but had never met her. Her husband at the time, Joe Case, had been doing weather on local TV in Nashville for years. We had so many mutual friends but yet we'd never met. Until. I had "stalked" Patrick Gottsch, the owner of RFD-TV long enough that he gave me a job at his AG network. I think it was just to shut me up. I knew it was destined to be. Not only because I was a farmer's daughter who did TV for a living, but I had an instant connection to those who worked there.

Pam had been hired by RFD-TV to be the executive producer for our news department and the shows Market Day Report and Rural Evening News. Within the first ten minutes of working together, we were locked in as friends. She was a Christian and wasn't shy about it. I loved that. She was a foodie and wasn't shy about it. Our friendship was quickly cemented. Since her husband Joe was an avid golfer, she was free on the weekends to do lunch, brunch, and have girl time. We became besties and brunch buddies.

She also helped me get my appearances on national cooking shows on TNT and the Food Network. It was a grueling process to get chosen to compete on these network shows. I would often have to go to Atlanta or other destinations to "audition" for these competitions. But with my schedule as an anchor at RFD-TV it was a challenge. Pam would literally rearrange recording times at RFD so that I could get on the road and make my audition time slot. She was my cheerleader from day one. Then, when

her husband became suddenly ill and unexpectedly passed away, we were devastated. I had actually been at their house the night before Joe passed to bring him some of his favorite dishes. Having no idea that would be my last time to see Joe. Hours later, he was gone. At the time of Joe's passing, I was already in the process of returning home to Monroe. I was still going to be working for RFD. But since part of my job was shooting and producing a show called Texas Agriculture Matters, I spent a lot of time in Texas. I also was the reporter covering all the big Ag conventions and farm shows. The owner of the network had agreed to let me move back home to Louisiana to be closer to family and just travel to wherever he needed me. But when Joe passed away, I seriously considered not moving home. I was so upset about Joe's passing and really thought I needed to stay in Nashville to be near Pam. But Pam assured me she was surrounded by family and friends, her faith was strong, and she would make it through this extremely difficult time. She did. What a strong woman of faith.

Not long after Joe passed, Pam went to her high school reunion and ran into her old boyfriend, Mick Bentley. Mick was divorced and he and Pam reconnected. It's such a touching love story. They were in love as teenagers. High School sweethearts reunited! They were able to reconnect after all these years, and now they're happily married. Mick is such gem, and they're so good together. Her friendship has meant the world to me.

Pam wanted to share a recipe for the book that is something that I would have never in a million years have thought to make or share. It's Mick's Ham Bone Soup recipe. And I also got Pam to contribute her cornbread recipe!

Devotion

The greatest testimony of a person's faith is not how loudly they worship when life is good, but how steadily they trust God when life breaks in two. We all walk through sorrow no one can fully prepare for, and yet God holds us up. Staying rooted in Jesus before the storm arrives is what prepares us when it does. The faith that carries us into grief is not the same faith that carries us through grief.

And God, in His tenderness, do not just sustain us, but He restores us. He writes a second chapter of love we can never imagine, not to erase the first, but to show that hearts can hold both memory and new joy at the same time. That is what redemption looks like when God authors the healing: something sweet growing out of something that once felt unbearable.

Some people God brings to you for reason, not always a season. Others He assigns to your soul for a lifetime.

SCRIPTURE (NIV):
"The Lord is close to the brokenhearted and saves those who are crushed in spirit."
— Psalm 34:18

PRAYER:
Lord, thank You for Your grace and loyalty to us. Your sustaining power gets us to the other side of tragedy, fear, and pain. Bless our new seasons of love, and continue to use us as a reminder that You heal, You restore, and You bless beyond what we can ever imagine. Help me cherish the friends who walk beside me through every season and turn and help me be a person who lights the way for others to see your divine healing. Amen.

Pam's Illegal Cornbread

1 can creamed corn
½ cup vegetable or corn oil
8 oz sour cream
2 eggs
2 cups self-rising corn meal
Pinch of sugar
Butter or margarine (optional)

Preheat oven to 385°F. Place seasoned iron skillet in oven while pre-heating (lightly grease skillet before placing in oven if skillet is not seasoned).

In large mixing bowl, spoon together the wet ingredients (eggs, corn oil and creamed corn). Add sour cream and mix thoroughly. Add cornmeal and mix until all corn meal is thoroughly blended with wet ingredients. Batter will be lumpy.

(Optional) Add a nice pinch of sugar to add slight sweetness in flavor.

Bake for 20-25 minutes until top of cornbread is golden brown, slightly crispy on the outside. Watch carefully in baking as some oven temperatures will vary.

Remove from oven and allow to sit for 5-10 minutes before cutting.

Cut & serve. Adding butter is optional as this recipe is extremely moist and tasty without it.

This recipe was shared with Pam from a dear friend in the 80s who worked in a downtown Nashville, Tennessee law office. The recipe was shared from one attorney to another for years and eventually landed in Pam's hands while she worked at a Nashville television station. Pam has never made another cornbread recipe since. This is her go-to every time, legal or not.

Bob Courtney

If you've known me since 1991, you know that I stepped away from riding horses to riding the Iron Ponies (motorcycles). Let me tell you how I transitioned from hooves to Harleys. It starts with a man, of course. I met Don Ragusa shortly after moving to Baton Rouge and started working as the co-host of the morning show at WBRZ. Don had me at hello. A man's man with an infectious laugh and a love for life and motorcycles. Our second date was on his Harley. I'd never ridden a motorcycle. Not as a passenger and definitely not as a driver. But I was hooked! I told Don, 'You're going to teach me how to drive a motorcycle." Because it was the closest sensation to riding a Cutting Horse as I'd ever experienced. Don said, "I'm not teaching someone who's never ridden before on my beloved bike." I said, "If you want to see me again, you will!"

The next weekend we went to a vacant parking lot in Baton Rouge, and for hours I did "figure eights." Don was such a great teacher, I never dropped the motorcycle once! Soon after, I took the motorcycle safety course and bought my first (of seven) Harley Davidsons! Don would end up breaking my heart a few years later, but I will forever be grateful to him for teaching me to ride. (Don and I ended up becoming great friends down the road.) Because it was my love of motorcycle riding that led me to Bob Courtney and TW Robinson (not her real name, but it's her TV name, so I'll stick with it.)

Meeting Bob is an interesting story in itself. You see, Bob Courtney and his wife, Beth, were giants in the Baton Rouge TV market. Before moving to Baton Rouge, I knew "of" two people in the TV business. They were legends. John Spain and Bob Courtney. They both worked at WBRZ in Baton Rouge. A powerhouse of a station. With the help of Leo Honeycutt, I got hired at WBRZ. I discovered that Bob left WBRZ about 30 days before I was hired on as anchor/reporter. Bob was legendary for his reporting. He departed WBRZ to become the First Assistant Louisiana Secretary of State under Fox McKeithen. In the summer of 2005, Fox died unexpectedly. My news director said I needed to go do a story on Fox McKeithen for the 6:00 o'clock news. He wanted the angle to be that Fox had a drinking problem and other demons that he couldn't wrestle to the ground. I said, "I will do a story on Fox but not from the negative angle. My thought was, Fox may have had a drinking problem, but he should be known for the good he did in this state, not for his addiction to alcohol".

So I left the newsroom in search of a positive story on Fox. I soon learned the employees of Secretary of State's office had been forbidden from speaking to the media. I was panicking. I needed an on-camera interview about Fox. It suddenly popped into my head that the Bob Courtney had recently quit the Secretary of State's office. He didn't have to abide by the gag order. He could talk. Bob had quit the Secretary of State's office a few months before launching a motorcycle travel show called La Rider. I called Bob's office and asked for an interview about our recently deceased Secretary of State Fox McKeithen. He said yes, come on over. This proved to be a meeting that would give birth to a friendship that is treasured to this day.

Bob, although a 'hard' newsman in his pre-La Rider days, agreed that McKeithen deserved to be remembered, at least in those first few hours after his death, for the good he had done. Not for his drinking problem. So I got my "positive" story on Fox and in return Bob got to know this TV person (me) who had a newfound love of motorcycle riding.

I resigned from WBRZ shortly after that. I started contributing to La Rider as a reporter and sometimes co-host. Not only did I get to know Bob, but this is where I met the vivacious TW Robinson. There aren't enough adjectives to describe how wonderful this woman is. She is a motorcycle queen. She will ride anything at any time. But the best part about TW is her personality. This woman is funny, smart, fearless, compassionate, and such a hoot to be around. What she lacked in TV polish in the early days of La Rider she made up for in passion and personality! (And she soon became a very polished television host!) There's absolutely no way I can have a "friends and family" section in this cookbook and not include them.

Bob didn't contribute a recipe, although I understand he's a fabulous cook. But I do know for a fact that he's a huge fan of my homemade toffee. So I'm including that recipe next.

Now for TW's recipe. When I reminded her that if she didn't contribute a recipe for my cookbook that she wouldn't be part of it, she said, "Oh okay, here's my best recipe."

She said, "When you get home with your Styrofoam box of leftovers, put it in the fridge. The next day, when hungry, you carefully open the Styrofoam box. Place contents on a microwave-safe dish. Heat but do not overheat. Enjoy! Discard Styrofoam box."

As you may have guessed, TW doesn't cook! But if you've ever watched our TV show, La Rider (you can find it in most TV markets in Louisiana or on Youtube under LaRiderTVBob.) you will quickly learn she does love to eat. It's amazing that she's not the size of a Volkswagon! She's much more disciplined than myself. She can eat a few bites of a bacon cheeseburger on camera and put it down and walk away. I, on the other hand, when I like something, I want to eat all of it!

Some of my best memories are of our two-wheeled adventures for La Rider. From the Strawberry Festival in Ponchatoula, Louisiana to the Tomato Place in Vicksburg, Mississippi, we've had some tasty travels. Thank you guys, for including me in your 'wind therapy' program. I love you to the beach and back.

English Toffee

1 cup unsalted butter
1¼ cups white sugar
2 tbsp water
¼ cup slivered almonds (optional)
1 cup chocolate chips

Put parchment paper in a 10x15" pan. I use glass.

Start by melting butter in a heavy skillet over medium heat. Stir in sugar and water, then bring to a boil. Stirring constantly, until sugar is golden. You'll cook to the hard crack stage which is 300° to 310°F. Pour mixture into the prepared pan; do not spread.

Let it cool for just a few minutes. Then sprinkle chocolate chips onto hot sugar mixture. Spread chocolate over the surface as it melts. If you like nuts on top, this is where you will chop the almonds and sprinkle them on top. Let cool completely before breaking into pieces.

Devotion

It's amazing how God uses what looks like one chapter in our lives to open the door to another, weaving a perfect quilt. Unfortunately for our comfort, it rarely unfolds the way we imagine.

Some of the most important friendships in our lives would never have existed if the first storyline had worked out. We think we lost something, but God knew we were actually being positioned. The Lord is a master weaver, and more than not we only understand His handiwork in reverse. What feels like heartbreak in one season turns out to be holy setup in the next.

That is the beauty of God's path. He uses the unexpected route. He uses the "I didn't see that coming" moments. When God is steering your story, even detours become destiny.

The road can seem bumpy, winding, and rough, but in God's map, no ground is wasted.

Sometimes the joy of a story isn't who was in the first chapter; it's what comes in chapter two.

SCRIPTURE (NIV):
"I will instruct you and teach you the way you should go; I will give you counsel and watch over you,"
— Proverbs 3:5-6

PRAYER:
Lord, thank You for turning detours into divine appointments and heartbreak into holy redirection. Thank You for the friendships and blessings that came out of roads I never expected to travel. Help me trust that when You close one door, You are already opening a better one — filled with purpose, people, and places I never would have found on my own. Amen.

The Garden:
Growing Health from the Ground Up

Hands in the soil, sunlight on your shoulders, the quiet hum of creation all around you. It's a place where peace and purpose grow side by side. Whether you're tending a few pots on the porch or a full backyard bed, gardening connects you to the rhythm of life and teaches one of the simplest truths: you reap what you sow.

Practical tips for growing healthy, abundant vegetables

Start Small and Steady. If you're new to gardening, begin with just a few plants. Herbs like basil, mint, or parsley, and vegetables like tomatoes, peppers, or lettuce are forgiving and rewarding. A few healthy plants will bring more joy (and produce!) than an overcrowded garden that's hard to manage. *Tip: Raised beds or large containers make it easier to control soil quality and drainage.*

Feed the Soil First. Healthy soil grows healthy plants. Mix in compost, aged manure, or organic matter at the start of each season. Good soil should smell rich and earthy, not sour or dry. *Tip: A simple rule of thumb is to feed your soil, not just your plants. The more alive your soil is, the less you'll need to rely on fertilizers.*

Water with Wisdom. Plants need deep, consistent watering. Early morning is best, before the heat of the day evaporates moisture. Avoid watering leaves late in the evening, which can invite mildew and pests. *Tip: A slow, steady soak at the base of the plant encourages roots to grow deep and strong.*

Choose the Right Companions. Just like people, plants have friends that help them thrive. Tomatoes love basil and marigolds. Carrots and onions grow well together. On the other hand, some plants compete, so it's worth checking a companion planting chart before sowing. *Tip: Mixing flowers like marigolds with your vegetables can naturally deter pests while adding color to your garden.*

Keep It Clean and Pruned. Remove dead leaves and weeds regularly to keep air flowing and prevent disease. Pinch off excess growth on tomatoes and herbs to encourage fuller, healthier plants. *Tip: Don't toss those trimmings. Instead, add them to your compost pile to give nutrients back to the earth.*

Rotate and Rest. Each season, rotate crops so the same vegetables aren't grown in the same spot year after year. This prevents soil depletion and discourages pests and diseases that target specific plants. *Tip: When the growing season ends, cover bare soil with mulch or a cover crop like clover to protect and enrich it through winter.*

Harvest with Gratitude. Pick vegetables when they're ripe: not too soon, not too late. Regular harvesting often encourages more growth. As you gather your produce, take a moment to notice what your hands have done. You planted, watered, waited, and nurtured. The garden rewards patience as much as effort. *Tip: The earlier you pick greens and herbs, the more flavorful and tender they'll be.*

Enjoy the Process, Not Just the Produce. Gardening is as much about peace of mind as it is about food on the table. The weeds will come, and so will the rain, but each season is a new beginning. You'll learn by watching, by failing, by trying again, and by succeeding. You and your garden's growth will take time.

With care, patience, and sunlight, it, and you, become something nourishing. When we tend our hearts the way we tend our gardens, with attention, rest, and gratitude, we grow stronger. So, plant your seeds, water your hope, and let your garden remind you that good things take effort and time to grow.

Jenifer Andrews

I'll say it again, I've been blessed to work with so many talented people throughout my career. A handful of those people have become dear friends, not just coworkers. Jenifer Andrews is one of them. We started working together at KTVE/KARD in Monroe. Then we worked together again at KNOE. She is such an incredible woman. For someone who talks for a living, she's probably the best listener in the world. She has heard me moan and groan about more "boy" troubles than I can count. And she's been able to give me relationship advice during a two minute commercial break while we're anchoring the 5:00pm news that's on point! She's also taken my teasing about her always "eating out of a box"! You know, those little square frozen meals you find in the freezer section at the grocery store? I just can't do it. For her, it's normal.

She wasn't raised in Louisiana, where cooking and eating are our national pastime! But I did my best to expand her palette. On some occasions, I did. But more than not, she passed my goodies on to her husband. I've learned that even though she says she's not a cook, she really can whip up something from scratch.

I did talk her into finding a recipe that she wanted to share. Jenifer is beautiful inside and out. I'm thankful our paths have crossed.

Devotion

We often think ministry looks like preaching or leading, but so often it looks like listening. A person who can absorb your tears during a commercial break and still throw to the next news story with composure is more than a coworker; that's a God-placed support beam in the architecture of your life.

Some people feed our bodies with food. Others feed our spirits with presence. And sometimes the one who brings comfort to the soul is just as nourishing as the one who brings a plate to the table. God places different gifts in different people so that we learn to recognize love in its many forms, not just the familiar ones.

That is a reflection of spiritual maturity: the ability to show up for another person, not always with answers, but with patience, compassion, and a shoulder strong enough to lean on.

The truest friends aren't the ones who share all your habits, they're also the ones who share your burdens.

SCRIPTURE (NIV):
"Be devoted to one another in love. Honor one another above yourselves."
— Romans 12:10

PRAYER:
Lord, thank You for the friends who carry us with compassion, who listen when our hearts are tired, and who reflect Your kindness through their steady presence. Help me to learn that Your comfort, strength, and companionship comes in many ways. Help me also to love others with the same patience and grace and attentiveness. Amen.

Jen's Juicy Chicken with Basil Sauce

1 chicken breast
½ cup chicken broth
1 tsp dried basil
¼ red bell pepper, chopped
1 small slice of onion
½ cup Parmesan cheese
1 Tbsp butter

Dip chicken in flour, then into a raw egg and again in the flour

Fry over medium heat

When done remove chicken and soften red pepper in the drippings, then add onions to carmelize

Add the chicken broth, parmesan cheese, basil and butter to the mixture along with flour to thicken

Pour sauce over the chicken.

Mint Tea

2 cups sugar
2 cups of water
6-8 sprigs of mint
1 cup orange juice
½ cup lemon juice
12 tea bags

Place 2 cups of sugar and 2 cups of water in a saucepan. Stir and boil for 5 minutes until sugar dissolves. Add 6-8 sprigs of mint and let it sit for 20 minutes. Squeeze and remove mint from the sugar/water mixture.

Separately, steep 12 regular-size tea bags in 1 quart very hot water. In a large bowl, add tea and the sugar/water mixture, then add 2 quarts cold water. Add 1 cup orange juice and ½ cup lemon juice. Mix all together. Makes 1 gallon. This tea lasts for up to 7 days. I use spearmint plant sprigs, and sometimes add orange and lemon mint sprigs.

Lynne Williams

I just love that I have met so many wonderful people and now lifelong friends through my connection to the Louisiana, Texas, and Tennessee Departments of Agriculture. Lynne Williams is the Fair Coordinator at the Tennessee Department of Agriculture. She's been helping me with stories for RFD-TV, the agriculture network, for as long as I can remember. She would often ask me to judge the pie contests at the Tennessee State Fair.

We became more than colleagues, we became friends. She has asked me to help her with some cookie decorating techniques. That is such a compliment!

So when the Friends and Family section of this cookbook was birthed, I knew Lynne needed to be a part. She's sharing a treasured family recipe for Mint Tea. But more importantly, she's sharing a part of her heart. Her late son loved this tea. For years, after losing him, she couldn't bring herself to make the tea. It was just too painful. It brought back too many memories. But she decided to share it with me. And make it again.

Please take the time to read the story in Lynne's own words while you sip some of this amazing mint tea and honor her late son, Thomas.

Devotion

When someone we love leaves this world, the heart takes time to relearn how to breathe around the empty space. For a while, even beautiful things can feel unbearable. But grief is not weakness; it is evidence of love that had deep roots.

Grief is not just about missing a person. It is about learning how to live in the spaces they once filled. Sometimes what hurts the most is not the big milestones, but the small things they loved: a song, a scent, a place… or a glass of mint tea. Something so simple can feel like too much, because memory isn't just remembered — it is felt.

Love does not disappear when someone is gone. It ripens. It deepens. It becomes legacy.

Often God brings us back to what we once avoided, not to reopen a wound, but to reveal that He has been gently mending it. The tears don't mean we're broken, they mean the memory still matters. That the love still lives abnd healing has begun.

And over time, grief transforms from pain at what was lost, into gratitude for what was had, and we transition into honoring the memory as we heal.

SCRIPTURE (NIV):
"The Lord heals the brokenhearted and binds up their wounds."
— Psalm 147:3

PRAYER:
Lord, thank You for the loved ones who touched our lives so deeply that their absence still echoes in our hearts. Continue to bring comfort, healing, and gentle restoration to all of us when we grieve. Remind me Lord to treasure the moments, the presence, and the memories that keep my heart connected to the people You gave us. Amen.

Mary's BBQ Brisket

1 large brisket trimmed
1 large bottle Worcestershire Sauce
¼ cup liquid smoke
1 garlic clove, minced
Black pepper to taste
Tony Cachere's seasoning to taste

Place brisket in a large pan cover with Worcestershire sauce and liquid smoke. Then spread the garlic all over the brisket and sprinkle with Tony's and pepper.

Preheat your oven to 275°F degrees. Make a double-layered aluminum foil pouch for the brisket: place two layers of foil down on the counter, place the brisket (with the fat side up) on the foil, and pull the edges of the foil up around the brisket to wrap it. The pouch needs to be sealed well so that it will keep in all of the moisture. Let the brisket sit (refrigerated) in the spice rub for 3 to 24 hours, or cook immediately.

Place the foil pouch on a baking sheet or baking dish and cook for 3 to 5 hours, depending on the size of your brisket.

Turn off the oven and allow the brisket to rest until it's cool enough to handle without oven mitts.

Pour the accumulated juices from the brisket into a large measuring cup or a bowl. Skim the fat from the juices, reserving the juices and saving 2 tablespoons of the fat for the sauce. Keep the brisket wrapped in foil and return it to the warm oven while you make the barbecue sauce.

Greg and Mary Clark

If you've lived in northeast Louisiana for any amount of time, you have no doubt been impacted by this dynamic Christian couple. You may not even know that you have, but you have. Their desire to love Jesus and to love people is unmatched. Greg pastors Cedar Crest Baptist Church in West Monroe. I met him years ago when we were waiting in line to volunteer at a Convoy of Hope food drive. (Greg always must remind me that's how we met because I have such a terrible memory!) We were instant friends. He introduced me to his beautiful wife, Mary. Again, fast friends. Mary even told me they used to watch me on the morning show in Baton Rouge, years before we met, when they lived in south Louisiana.

No matter where I've lived, they've always kept in touch with me. Always prayed for me. The crazy thing is, I've never officially been a member of Cedar Crest Baptist Church, but I do look to Greg as my pastor.

One of the most amazing things they helped me with is to fulfill a God-given dream to take a vacation with a purpose. Here's how it happened. It was a divine appointment that I attended a CCBC service while home one weekend from Nashville. During that service, a youth group from the non-profit Christian organization 410 Bridge was there. This group was from Kenya, Africa. I learned that day that a major part of the 410 Bridge ministry is teaching residents in some of the poorest parts of Kenya to farm. To grow their own food. Since I worked for the agriculture network, this was such an incredible opportunity to be able to share the gospel and do ag-centric stories for my network RFD-TV. But here was the craziest thing about that trip. I was very limited in the time I could take off from RFD. I had just a small window to take a vacation that year, and that window was only weeks away. Planning international travel usually takes months. But with Greg and Mary's connections at 410 Bridge and God's ability to make things happen, I was on a 19-hour flight to Nairobi literally weeks after that first conversation about 410 Bridge!

On the ground in those remote regions of Africa, I got to see firsthand God at work, through agriculture. Where I saw desolation and poverty, God saw people rich in love and compassion. I met these folks who had so little in the way of possessions but were so filled with joy. They were now learning to farm in one of the most challenging areas of the world to grow things. I saw more happiness exuding from these people who had little to nothing because they possessed the love of Jesus! With guidance and help from Ag and water experts with 410 Bridge, these residents were not only feeding their families but now they had businesses, an income. They were making a living! Their lives were being transformed.

I encourage you to check out 410 Bridge. Based on the scripture verse 1 Peter 4:10 "Each of you should use whatever gift you have received to serve others, as faithful stewards of God's grace in its various forms." www.410bridge.org

The 410 Bridge is a Christ-centered, non-profit organization helping to redefine the war on poverty through community development in poverty-stricken nations such as such as Kenya, Guatemala, Indonesia, Nicaragua, Uganda, and the Dominican Republic.

Greg. Mary. Thank you!! You have my heart.

Mary shared the brisket recipe on the previous page! Enjoy!

Devotion

When God writes a calling on your life, He doesn't just place people around you; He places people ahead of you, already walking the path you were meant to step into, and ready to help you with their knowledge.

People can activate us into the doing. They can awaken a purpose that sometimes we hadn't even acknowledged yet. Once you arrive, you witness a truth and the wealth of peace that can only come from Christ.

This is the transformation Scripture speaks of about discipleship, not giving resources to people, but restoring or awakening the God-given capacity within them.

One Sunday service, introduction, or yes, and suddenly, people across the world are moved into action because you were willing to share where He has brought you.

When we live open-handedly before God, our "small yes" can become someone else's breakthrough.

SCRIPTURE (NIV):
"Each of you should use whatever gift you have received to serve others, as faithful stewards of God's grace in its various forms."
— 1 Peter 4:10 (NIV)

PRAYER:
Lord, thank You for calling us to a life bigger than ourselves. A life of service, compassion, and obedience to Your leading. Bless the vessels of Your purpose, and bless the hands and hearts of those around the world who are learning to flourish through Your provision. Help me continue to use the gifts You've placed in me to build others up, here and wherever You send me next. Amen.

Billy Ray's Scrambled Eggs

2 large eggs
2 slices American cheese
¼ cup evaporated milk
2 Tbsp butter
Salt and pepper to taste

Heat up a cast iron skillet to medium high heat. Melt butter in the skillet.

In a bowl, beat the two eggs, add evaporated milk. Slice or tear the cheese slices into strips and add to the eggs. Once the skillet is hot, pour in the egg mixture. Immediately start moving the eggs around with a spatula or fork.

The secret to Daddy's scrambled eggs is they never "browned" on the bottom and got dried out. Continue to cook the eggs for just a few more minutes. Do not overcook. They should still be a bit "runny" but completely cooked through. Daddy knew exactly when to take them out of the skillet.

Salt and pepper the eggs. Just a side note: Daddy would cook our toast in that same cast iron skillet. Butter on each side until golden and crispy. That's the way to start the day!

Ken Booth

If you lived in northeast Louisiana between the 1970's and the 1990's you got your news from KNOE-TV. One of the best investigative journalists at that time was Ken Booth. Legendary for his relentless pursuit of all things right. There wasn't a crooked politician or shady businessman who didn't shake in their boots when they saw Ken Booth and his cameraman knocking on their door!

I'll never forget the day I met Ken. I was only a sophomore at Northeast Louisiana University (now ULM) majoring in Radio/TV/Broadcasting. I'd known since I was 16 that I wanted to be an anchor/reporter. My Mama's prayers of "Lord, I hope she gets paid for talking!" were answered when I walked into KNOE TV in Monroe in 1981 and asked for a job. Funny thing though, when I walked into the reception area without an appointment or knowing a soul, I actually asked to see Lanny James, the Sports Director. I was a huge sports fan. I loved watching football. I loved to play basketball and tennis and was learning the game of golf. I thought sports were where I needed to be. But you have to understand, this was way before ESPN and "girls" just didn't do sports. So on this day, the receptionist said Lanny wasn't in but Ken Booth was. Ken was the News Director, not just an investigative reporter. So I told the receptionist, okay, I'll see Ken. I was so ready to start my career, and I wasn't leaving until I talked to someone in charge! I didn't want to wait until I got my college degree.

I followed that black and white checkered hallway to Ken's office. He was sitting in his chair, cowboy boots perched on his desk and a cigarette dangling from his mouth. (This was 1981, so you could smoke anywhere you pleased back then!). Ken looked at me and with no small talk, asked, "What do you want?" I said I know this is what I was put on this earth to do. My 19-year-old self said, "This is what I can do and want to do, and you need to let me go ahead and start doing it!" Before responding, Ken took a big drag off his cigarette and without any further discussion, said, "I don't know why I'm doing this but I'm impressed with your guts to walk in my office, straight off the street and ask for it, so I'm giving you a job. You start tomorrow." Wow! I was both excited and scared to death.

I was a full-time college student, so my schedule at KNOE was working at night and helping prepare the 10:00p news. This is where I would meet some lifelong friends. (All of whom deserve their own chapters and recipes in this book! From John Denison and Judy Wagoner to Leo Honeycutt, Angie DeBlieux, Devon O'Day, Sailor Jackson, Bill Elliott and several more. KNOE was a powerhouse of TV and radio news in North Louisiana. Back when you could be a real journalist and just tell the stories as they really happened. I learned so much from all of them.

But one of the biggest things I learned was how to be a good anchor. I'll never forget my first night of going live on the air. After several weeks of just helping John and Judy get scripts, video, and "graphics" together—remember this was before everyone had a computer on their desk. We would pull "slides", like those that were used in school to project an image up on the wall, except these slides became an "over the

Ken Booth (continued)

shoulder" graphic when the news anchor was reading. That was my first job at KNOE. Pulling slides.

I begged Ken every day to let me do more. I wanted to be on the air. So he said I could do the 15-second news promo for the 10:00p.m. newscast one night. Something Judy or John normally anchored. It would air around 9:00p.m. telling viewers what big story would be coming up. I was so excited. The promo actually read like this: "Two people were killed in a small crash tonight in Richland Parish. Details coming up at ten." And I said that with the biggest smile on my face. Yep, grinning from ear to ear about two people dying in a plane crash! I was so excited to be on TV that I channeled my perfect pageant smile instead of paying attention to what I was saying. Ken scolded me immediately. Judy and John both said, "You have to not just read your scripts before you go on air, you have to read them. The folks at home need to feel like you're in their living room telling them the story and that you care about what you're saying. It's not about your face on camera. It's about the information and how it impacts their life and community." Fortunately, Ken didn't fire me for delivering tragic details with such insensitivity. He allowed me to learn from my mistake. And I did.

One other side note about Ken. Ken was a tough guy. He could be pretty gruff at times. But he also had a sensitive side. I got to see that first hand. Shortly after starting work at KNOE I began dating Randy Deaton, a KNOE radio DJ and Program Director. Randy was 12 years older than me and had a small child from a previous marriage. My father basically forbade me to

marry him. Telling me that I would be miserable and I was not prepared at 19 years old to be a stepmother. Daddy said he would not walk me down the aisle at my wedding. I was so hurt. Ken stepped up. He said I'll stand in for your father if you want me to. I thought that was so sweet. It ended up that my dad, two days before I was going to get married, called me and said. Okay, if you insist on marrying this guy, I'll walk you down the aisle. And Billy Ray Arender did... crying like a baby the entire time because he knew I was making a mistake. (Sure enough that marriage only lasted 2 ½ years. Daddy always knows best. My sincerest apologies to Randy and his daughter Gabrielle for not being the wife or stepmother I should have been!)

Finding a recipe to go along with Ken Booth was a bit of a challenge. Ken had passed by the time I decided to write this. And to be honest, I never saw the man eat a morsel of food. So I asked my friend Myra, who knew Ken well long after I left KNOE, if she knew any of his favorite foods. She asked his daughter and said he loved Snickers and scrambled eggs (not together).

So I decided to include my daddy's best scrambled eggs. They were the best. Just ask Christi Goss Purvis! Growing up, we ate our weight of Daddy's scrambled eggs with cheese when she would spend the night with me. They aren't just regular ole scrambled eggs.

Devotion

We should want people in our lives who challenged us, sharpened us, and see the potential before we have fully grown into it. That is what true mentors do. They are the gatekeepers God uses to usher us into purpose. They don't make us comfortable, but that is where God works most. Integrity in truth matters more than compliments.

God often uses people who seem tough on the outside to shape the gentleness, wisdom, and discernment inside of us. Sometimes the gruffest people are the ones who make the greatest deposits in our destiny, because they care more about who we become than whether we feel flattered along the way.

And look how God reveals his heart! The same man who barks orders could also stand in as a father when yours could not. The same woman who challenges you to complete the book you started, stands in as your cheerleader when you didn't have one. Under the hard edges you find a tenderness they didn't advertise, but lived when it mattered.

Not every mentor feeds us with good vibes. Some propel us with discomfort and growth.

SCRIPTURE (NIV): *"As iron sharpens iron, so one person sharpens another."*
— Proverbs 27:17

PRAYER:
Lord, thank You for the mentors who shape us , even the tough ones who refine our character, our calling, and our confidence. Thank You for the people who believed in us before we fully knew how to believe in ourselves. Bless the imprint they leave, and help me carry forward the same integrity, heart, and courage when I need it to be that for others. Amen.

Sourdough Bread

4¾ cups bread flour
   (or more as needed)
3 Tbsp white sugar
2½ tsp salt
0.25 oz package active dry yeast
1 cup warm milk
2 Tbsp margarine, softened
1½ cups sourdough starter
1 extra large egg
1 Tbsp water

Start by mixing together 1 cup flour, sugar, salt, and yeast in a large bowl. Add warm milk and margarine. Stir in the sourdough bread starter. Add in remaining 3¾ cups flour gradually.

Flour your counter or work surface. Turn dough out onto the flour dusted surface and knead for 8 to 10 minutes. Place dough into a greased bowl, turn once to oil surface, and cover. Allow to rise until doubled in size, about 1 hour.

Using your fist, Punch down dough; cover and let rest for 15 minutes. Divide dough in half and shape into 2 loaves. Place loaves on a greased baking pan. Allow to rise until doubled in volume, about 1 hour.

Preheat the oven to 375°F

Stir together egg and water in a small bowl. Brush over the tops of loaves.

Bake in the preheated oven until loaves are golden brown and cooked through, about 30 minutes. An instant-read thermometer inserted into the center of a loaf should read 190°F.

Al Tompkins

There is hardly a day goes by while living in Nashville that I don't think of Al Tompkins. He was a longtime news director at WSMV, the NBC affiliate, not to mention a multi award-winning journalist, author and speaker. He was the first one to take a chance on this little Louisiana girl and give her a shot in the big city of Nashville.

It's really a God story how it all happened. Right down to God orchestrating pregnancies! (Let me explain.)

I knew early on that I wanted to live in Nashville. I fell in love with this city as a kid. Our parents brought us to Opryland Theme Park (a mini–Disney World that no longer exists **sigh**). There were country music shows and rides. Plus, the Grand Ole Opry. We loved country music at our house. My sister and I would both sing with the vacuum cleaner hose in hand to Loretta Lynn's Coal Miner's Daughter for hours! So, for country music fans, Nashville was a mecca. I had set my sights on moving to Music City one day. After about 5 years of doing the morning show in Baton Rouge at WBRZ, I had decided I was ready for the big TV market of Nashville.

Prior to landing my first job in NashVegas (another little moniker for Music City), I had started finagling my way to Nashville for "assignments." Talking my news directors (whoever I was working for—be it Monroe, Little Rock or Baton Rouge) into letting me go to Nashville to cover the big country music awards shows. There was always a local connection. I was never an investigative-type reporter until I needed to find a legitimate reason to go to Nashville for work!

Every time I made a trip, I was always armed with a box of resume tapes. (Again, pre-YouTube and Vimeo links!).

I was never successful in getting in to see any of the news directors. Or, more specifically, any of the powers that be at the then Nashville Network, home to the famed Crook and Chase show. I just knew I was going to be the next Lorianne Crook! But on my third or fourth trip, I made it past the receptionist at WSMV. Al Tompkins, the news director, agreed to see me. I was getting my first Nashville TV station interview! Yay! I handed Al my resume tape. He popped it in the VHS machine. He turns to face the TV monitor on the wall so that I'm looking at the back of his head. Al proceeds to look at my snipits of anchoring, reporting, and live shots. I'm thinking I'm pretty good. Hey, I've been doing TV now for about 12 years! "Heck, I was surprised Good Morning America hadn't called me!" I thought with all the humility I could muster. But just minutes in and Al starts ripping apart my work. He didn't like my hair (which was always an issue with the news director. I liked myself with long hair. Back then, before Fox and Friends, the short little "bob" haircuts were the industry standard for news anchors.) He didn't like my writing, and he wasn't even impressed with my "live" reports. And "live," out in the field, is where I shined.

When Al ejected the tape and swung back around to face me, I had tears streaming down my face. I felt so hurt and deflated. I came in with my best work and was basically told I had chosen the wrong profession. (Al remembers it quite differently. He viewed it as *constructive criticism. He's even sincerely apologized for making me cry.) With a shaky voice and through tears, I thanked Al for his time and said, "Well, I'm lucky they love me in Baton Rouge!" That was in October 1993, I think. Three months later, in January 1994 I quit my job at WBRZ. I sold my house, Harley Davidson and every stick of furniture I owned to move to Nashville without a job to not be a country music singer! (Like most folks who sell all of their belongings and move to Music City!) But I had prayed and knew beyond a shadow of a doubt that I was supposed to be in Nashville.*

So, with what could fit in the trunk of my car, I called my friend Angie DeBlieux Bryan and asked, "Girl, can I crash at your house for a few days until I can find an apartment?" I had worked with Angie at KNOE and she remains a dear friend to this day. She said yes to my new address! With what little money I had in the bank, I rented a tiny apartment downtown on the Cumberland River. I think it was all of 537 square feet. I had nothing but a mattress, an answering machine, a coffee pot, and box of resume tapes! I did my best to get interviews at The Nashville Network and all of the affiliates in Nashville. No luck. Not one news director or general manager agreed to see me. What I did do on that first Monday I moved to Music City was call Al Tompkins. I told him that I had moved to Nashville and was ready to work. He asked, "You quit and moved to Nashville without a job to go to?" I said, "Yes sir, because there is no one in this town running circles around me, including Demetria Kalodimos!" Demetria was the longtime and well-respected anchor

at WSMV. And honestly, she was running circles around me, but I was not about to let Al know that!

Nearly six weeks passed and not one nibble from a TV station. I had very little money in the bank. I may have sold everything I owned except my car, but it took most of that money to pay off my debt. I had promised Daddy that I wouldn't ask him for help. As you can imagine, my father was not keen on the idea of me moving to the big city without a job. I started scanning the want ads in the newspaper. I needed income. I was not tucking tail and moving back to Louisiana. Despite being destitute and unemployed I was convinced God had brought me there for a reason.

I answered an ad in the Tennessean to be the desk clerk at the Hermitage Hotel in downtown Nashville. I had been a huge fan of the TV show "Hotel" which starred James Brolin and Connie Seleca. And I thought, hey, if I can't do TV, I can work in hospitality and meet some very interesting people at this posh hotel. I aced the interview with hotel management, even though the head honcho was a bit skeptical that I really wanted to work for minimum wage at a hotel. My resume clearly stated I was a TV and Radio person. But I snowed, I mean convinced her. She said, "You're hired." She sent me to be fitted for my hotel "uniform" and take the drug test. I was going to start training the following Monday.

But that night after passing my drug test, which I passed with flying colors by the way, I got home to my empty apartment and saw a blinking light on the answering machine. One message. From Al Tompkins.

Al Tompkins (continued)

Al said, "Hey, I've got a reporter that's leaving to go on maternity leave. I can give you a reporting job, but when she comes back to work in 8 weeks, you're out." I said, "Yes, I'll do it!" I called the manager at the Hermitage Hotel and told her she was right. I wanted to do television. Begged her forgiveness and then called everyone back home to tell them I had my first TV job in Nashville! My Mom and Dad were so happy. I think more so for the fact that I wouldn't be asking for money than for my career move!

True to his word, Al let me know that the reporter who had the baby was about to come back from maternity leave. I'd be out on the street. But to my amazement, the News Director at WKRN, the ABC affiliate, and Al had talked. I didn't know at the time but learned that Al had actually called Bob Mueller, the interim News Director at the competing TV station, mind you, and said, "You need to take a look at this reporter. I no longer have a position for her, but she's got something." So Bob mentions to Al that he has a reporter going on maternity leave. She was leaving that next week. So Al connected me with Bob Mueller. I walked out of WSMV on a Friday and into WKRN on Monday. With the same terms and conditions, when that reporter would return in 8 weeks from maternity leave, I'd be out of job. Then the real crazy thing happened. I was about to be booted from WKRN because the reporter was returning from maternity leave, when Al Tompkins called. He said, "I just had a reporter quit. Come back to WSMV and I can offer you a full-time position." I said, tongue in cheek, "Really?! Is this the same person who, just a

few months earlier, thought I was not fit to be in TV News?" Al replied, "Well you obviously learned a lot under my tutelage! Al was right. I learned more in my 8 weeks under him as news director, than I did in my first 12 years in broadcasting. That man is a genius when it comes to reporting and writing and overall good storytelling. He went on to write the book, "Aim for The Heart", a book that transformed the way I shoot and write stories for TV. I encourage anyone in the TV news business to get it. I actually bought several and gave them away to young reporters.

Now back to my career! I told Bob Mueller and the general manager at WKRN, Mike Sechrist, that Al wanted me to come back to WSMV. Since my job was about to end at News 2, I didn't think it would be problem. I was a freelancer. Not under contract, so I could legally station hop. But Sechrist, he and I got along well. Sechrist seemed to really like my reporting and anchoring. Plus, I had filled in on the anchor desk a time or two for Anne Holt. Sechrist said, "We don't want you to go back across the street. What would it take for you stay here at NEWS 2?" And I said, "I really want to anchor. Not just be a reporter." At the time, Anne Holt was the main anchor at WKRN. A beautiful and talented news anchor who had made it clear she wasn't going anywhere for a while. But Mike and Bob told me they could move the weekend anchor to mornings and make me the weekend anchor. I said yes! Then I had to tell Al I wasn't coming back to WSMV. He was mad for a minute, but when I said, "You can offer me Demetria's job, and I'll come to you!" No surprise that didn't happen.

Al didn't stay mad long. He understood I needed to do what was right for my career. I would go on to anchor weekends and fill in for Anne Holt for the next 5 plus years at WKRN. I was so honored to work with some amazing people there. From Matthew Zelkind to Mike Sechrist, Joe Dubin and Jerry Barlar and SO many more. Too many to mention by name. But know that you all had an impact on my life!

That is how my career began in Nashville. Thanks to God, pregnancies, and Al Tompkins. I was blessed not only to work at WKRN and WSMV but also did some freelance work for Entertainment Tonight, The Nashville Network, Access Hollywood, and CBS This Morning. Plus, I became a contributor for the PBS show Tennessee Crossroads. I've been doing Tennessee Crossroads now for nearly 30 years!

When I asked Al for a recipe, he said he didn't have any family recipes to share, but he loves grilled cheese and tomato soup! He's got a God story to go along with. You've got to read it.

Al, still having an impact on my life. He works for The Poynter Institute, pouring into the lives of journalists around the world! Thank you, Al! The world is a better place because of you!

"When I think of my "favorite" food, I think of the food that comforts me, that reminds me of the meaningful moments of life. When I was a younger man, I might have chosen a fancy meal at a restaurant with linen tablecloths and waiters who wore gloves. Earlier this year, I saw a place in New York City that was charging $329 for a steak, the potato was extra. I could not focus on what was likely a wonderful meal, I was stuck on the price and all the good that could be done with that money.

Thank goodness I grew up and grew out of the fancy food phase. Today, my favorite meal, a meal I could enjoy every day is grilled cheese and tomato soup. And I know why.

When one of the four kids in my family was sick and had to stay home from school, my mother would always do two things to make us feel better. She would bring home a comic book, and she would make a grilled cheese and tomato soup. It made feeling rotten feel better.

One of my dearest friends passed away a month ago, and when Tammi asked me to write about a food that meant something to me, I thought of my friend. Rosie Oeschger was 93 years old and was a middle child of a family with eight children. She was born to Hungarian and Italian parents. About once a month, Rose and I would huddle for lunch, and she would tell me stories about her life and her total dedication to serving God.

I would usually start the conversation by saying, "Tell me a story you have never told me before." On this particular day, we sat down at a café that served soup and sandwiches, the sandwiches made with homemade bread. Each sourdough slice was at least a half inch

Al Tompkins (continued)

thick with a slice of gooey cheddar holding it together.

"When I was growing up," Rose said quietly, "My mother made bread like that every day. It was heavy and dense, and she sliced it thick like that. Everyone loved that Hungarian bread, but not me."

I leaned in to listen, knowing this was going to be a story that would contain a life lesson. Rose explained that around that time in rural Pennsylvania, people were starting to buy sliced white bread that came in sacks from the grocery store. Only poorer children, like her, brought homemade bread for the school lunches.

Rose said that she eagerly traded her homemade sandwiches for those thin-sliced white bread sandwiches, which the privileged children eagerly gave up for the delicious sandwiches in Rose's paper sack.

"You know," she continued, "The word bread is mentioned 492 times in the Bible. It is referred to as a source of nourishment for the body, but also for the soul. Jesus said, 'I am the bread of life' and the Lord's Prayer mentions our plea that God provide us 'our daily bread.'"

Since I was leaning over a grilled cheese, I asked, "Does the Bible mention cheese?"

"Yes," she said three times, twice in the books of Samuel and once in Job. It was not called cheese but curds, but it is the same thing."

When you sit down to your daily bread, be thankful for the simple things. Jesus didn't eat a $329 steak for his last meal. But we know he had bread. He broke it and said, "Eat, all of you, and remember me." – Al Tompkins

Devotion

It's very easy to feel rejected by a closed door or lost opportunity. However, God will swing open the right door after every other door is shut. That's His specialty! When we realize that, we no longer need to feel that shut doors are rejection, since we know God is mapping our steps. And what looks, in the beginning, like criticism and rejection may actually be God's way of sharpening your gift and preparing you for a platform you weren't quite ready to stand on yet.

We often pray for opportunity, but God first gives training, sometimes wrapped in discomfort, humbling moments, or people who tell us the truth with blunt honesty. The refining almost always comes before the release.

Only the Lord can orchestrate something so grand, in hindsight, that we can do nothing but give Him the glory.

This is what it means when Scripture says that "your gift will make room for you." A calling doesn't need to be forced when we let God Himself do the arranging. Your job isn't to have the perfect résumé, hair, or timing, Your job is to show up in faith and not give up.

And most times God doesn't just answer a dream, He custom-builds the route to it. We simply have to trust and follow.

SCRIPTURE (NIV):
"A person's gift makes room for them and brings them before great people." — Proverbs 18:16

PRAYER:
Lord, thank You for orchestrating our lives and purposes long before we see them ourselves. Thank You for mentors who sharpen, challenge, and push us closer to the calling You designed us for. Help me remember that every door You open is on purpose and on time, as well as every door You shut. Help me walk in the peace, knowing You are in control. Amen.

Vanilla Ice Cream

14 oz can sweetened condensed milk
2 tsp pure vanilla extract or vanilla bean paste
1 pinch fine salt
2 cups heavy cream, cold

In a cold metal bowl, combine the condensed milk, salt and vanilla.

In a bowl of a stand mixer whip the cream with the whisk attachment on medium-high speed until firm peaks form, about 2 minutes.

Fold about 1 cup of the whipped cream into the condensed milk mixture with a rubber spatula.

Then, fold the lightened mixture into the whipped cream until well blended.

Pour into a chilled 9x5x3" metal loaf pan, and freeze, covered, until thick and creamy, about for at least 5 hours.

Jan Hopkins Nolan

When I think about growing up on "Round Away Road, or Route 3 in Madison Parish, I am flooded with childhood memories. Actually, that's not true. My long-term memory is horrible.

That hurts my heart that I can't remember them all because I believe I was incredibly blessed to grow up in that little farming area also known as the Montrose community. Everyone out there farmed. My dad grew cotton and soybeans. Our neighbors farmed cotton, soybeans and, I guess, there was also corn? But I remember those fields of white gold in the fall and the miles and miles of what looked like green velvet, soybeans. Those soybeans would turn the most beautiful rust color when it came time to harvest.

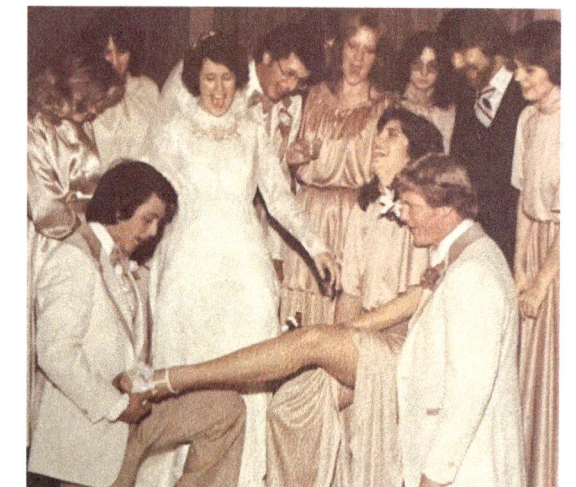

One of those neighbors, across the bayou and about a ½ a mile up the road, was Jan Hopkins. Daughter of Helen and Warren. She was a couple of years older than me. But she let me hang out with her, nonetheless! I would ride my three-wheeler or horse down to her house. She was the coolest. Jan was my first idol. I don't mean idol in a bad way. But in those tween years where I'm first starting to notice boys, pay attention to how I dressed, and starting to decide there's more to life than horses and hay bales, Jan was the one I looked up to. I loved going to her house. It was my first introduction to learning how to decorate my room. I distinctly remember her bedroom door having a beaded curtain. You know, those strings of beads that went from the top of the door to the floor? I begged my mom to let me get a beaded curtain for my doorway. I wanted to be like Jan.

Jan fell in love with Marty Nolan, a local Tallulah boy. They were certainly a match made in heaven. They had eyes only for each other. Jan had to remind me that when they got married, I sang at their wedding! What?! Me sing in public? I can sing in the shower and sing in the choir, but a solo in public, I choke. But I guess that's how much I loved Jan and she loved me. Because I agreed to sing at her wedding. I don't think I've ever told Jan how much her friendship meant to me. Love you, girl!

Her recipe is for her daddy's favorite homemade no-churn ice cream is on the previous page.

Devotion

There are some people we meet in childhood who help form us. Before we fully understand who we are, God often gives us someone a little bit ahead of us to look up to, and often they are our first living example of what confidence, kindness, or grace can look like. It could be a mother, father, sibling, or neighbor.

What makes this type of relationship sacred is that it often leaves marks on us that last a lifetime. We remember how they made us feel safe, included, inspired, and welcomed. Long before we know what "mentors" or "role models" are, they become just that. God weaves ordinary people into our story who teach us how to dream, find beauty, and learn to grow into ourselves.

Even decades later, their love and impression remain with us, because real influence never expires. You may not even remember every detail of your childhood, but you remember the love, which means the purpose of that connection did exactly what God intended.

God is that way with us. While we aren't always as "close" to Him as we feel, He is still leaving an impression on us that lasts a lifetime. We don't always remember a specific Scripture or exact biblical story, but it's there in our hearts to help encourage and guide us into becoming who we are meant to be.

SCRIPTURE (NIV):
"Encourage one another and build each other up..."
— 1 Thessalonians 5:11

PRAYER:
Lord, thank You for the people You placed in my life early on who shaped me before I even knew I was being shaped. The kindness, warmth, and influence they carried in those childhood years made me feel safe, seen, and loved. Help me never to overlook the quiet ways You form us through others and Your word. Teach me, Lord, how to be that blessing for someone else. Amen.

Following, you'll find some of my other almost-famous desserts. What secured my first national TV food competition was my White Chocolate Cheesecake with Praline Sauce. It was a TV show called "On the Menu." It starred Emeril Lagasse and Ty Pennington. I got runner-up. It was so much fun, especially when Emeril said my cheesecake was one of the best he's ever had!

Lady Godiva White Chocolate Cheesecake with Praline Sauce

Crust:
2⅔ cups vanilla wafers
1 Tbsp sugar
2 Tbsp butter, melted and cooled
1 tsp vanilla
½ cup pecans, toasted

Cake:
16 oz. cream cheese, softened
1 can condensed milk
½ cup sour cream
¼ cup sugar
2 eggs
2 egg yolks
¼ cup Lady Godiva White Chocolate Liqueur
1 tsp vanilla

Sauce:
½ cup light brown sugar
½ cup heavy cream
¼ cup butter
1 cup pecans
2 tsp vanilla

Preheat your oven to 325°F.

In a small food processor, combine vanilla wafers, sugar butter and pecans. Pulse until all cookies are now crumbs. Spray springform pan with nonstick cooking spray until bottom is completely covered. Put in freezer for 10 or 15 minutes to set.

In a large bowl, beat cream cheese til fluffy and smooth. Slowly add the condensed milk til completely combined. Add eggs, yolks and sugar and liqueur, vanilla and sour cream. Pour into cold crust. Bake in water bath. Bake at 325°F 35 to 40 minutes. It should still jiggle in the center.

Remove from the oven and let cool completely before putting it in the fridge. Then chill for at least 4 hours

Praline sauce:

mix brown sugar, cream, and butter and bring to boil. Boil 3 minutes, stirring constantly. Turn off heat and stir in pecans and vanilla..

This is the old fashioned kind of cheesecake, like the kind served in fine restautants. It requires a little more work, however, it is very worth the time and effort.

Ginger Crinkle Cookies

⅔ cup vegetable oil
1 cup sugar
1 egg
¼ cup molasses
2 cups all-purpose flour
½ tsp salt
1 tsp baking soda
1 tsp ground cinnamon
½ tsp ground ginger
¼ cup sugar

Combine oil and 1 cup sugar in a large bowl. Add egg and beat well. Stir in molasses. Combine flour, salt, soda, cinnamon and ginger. Add to molasses mixture. Stir well.

Roll into 1-inch balls, roll each ball in remaining ¼ cup sugar. Place on greased cookie sheet. Bake at 350°F for 8 to 10 minutes for chewy cookies. Another minute for more crisp cookies.

I love a ginger snap... but without the snap! So I will be forever grateful when a dear friend from Baton Rouge, Dana Watkins McKearn, shared with me a chewy ginger molasses cookie recipe one Christmas.

From Tammi

This will be the shortest chapter for sure! Each January 1, like everyone else, vow to get off the sugar and carbs. Then January 3 rolls around and I'm off the wagon! And everyone asks me why I don't develop some healthy variations of all my desserts. So I try. I buy the almond flour, sugar substitute, the applesauce and all the ingredients that make a dish sugar-free, fat-free, and taste-free! Because the taste and texture is never the same, I end up throwing it out. And that crushes me because all those 'healthy' ingredients are expensive. So I've decided I'd rather try to 'just say no' to eating sugar and carbs than eat something I don't like. That's just me.

I do wish I had been more disciplined with my eating habits throughout my life. I've lost a couple of dream jobs because I was overweight. One of those was with Entertainment Tonight, the TV news show based out of Hollywood, about celebrities. I was freelancing for them as a producer in Nashville. Meaning they would hire me to go do interviews with people in Nashville like Garth Brooks, Johnny and June Cash, Reba McEntire, and even Whitney Houston. Interviewing Whitney was a highlight. It was just a few months before she died.

I would do the interviews, and you would see my hand holding the microphone on Entertainment Tonight, but never my face. Sometimes they would even fly in "talent" to front the piece as opposed to letting me do it. I finally asked my boss at ET, what gives? I am an anchor and reporter here in Nashville. Being on camera is what I do. He looked me straight in the eye and said lose 20 pounds and you can do it. I was too fat to be on camera. I felt so dejected.

Of course, I immediately started a diet. I was in my 30s, exercised like a fiend and ate like a bird. But I couldn't sustain it. I love food, rich, decadent, fabulous-tasting food. I think I lost 10 pounds, but it wasn't enough. I put it right back on.

So I understand what the disciple Paul meant when he said he "had a thorn in his side." My eating disorder has been my thorn. It's been the thing my entire life that has kept me from being everything God wanted me to be. Not that being a reporter for Entertainment Tonight was the end all be all, but it meant that I let my taste buds rule my life. My weird eating habits have also impacted relationships because I wouldn't eat past 6:00p or once I got hungry, I had to eat right then. I do apologize to my friends and family for being so whack-adoo with my eating. Please forgive me. I'm embarrassed that I haven't yet turned that over to God and let Him heal me of that disorder. That's on me. Not God.

Devotion

There are some battles that don't happen out in the open; they live quietly inside of us, where old shame and silent struggle meet. Food may seem like a small thing to the world, but when something becomes a source of identity, comfort, or control, it stops being about calories and starts being about the soul. That is why some battles we face feel so heavy. It's not because you are weak, but because it has been spiritual as much as physical.

Most of us wrestle with public sins, as well as private ones. The private ones are like thorns that no one else fully sees but that never fully go away. Paul prayed for his to be removed, and God did not take it away… instead, He gave grace that carried him through it. Sometimes the thorn isn't an enemy; it becomes a tether that keeps us reaching for Jesus instead of ourselves.

Read this carefully: your worth was never tied to a clothing size, a camera angle, or a casting decision.

Your calling was never revoked because of your struggle.

And your testimony will only become deeper, not weaker, with every battle.

You do not fail because you still struggle. You show courage because you refuse to hide from God.

Healing rarely begins when we "fix" something; it begins when we finally stop trying to fix it alone. The Lord is only asking you for surrender in the struggle, not strength. Only grace changes what willpower can only temporarily manage.

You have not failed God in this. If anything, this is the very place where He is waiting to accept and love you most tenderly.

SCRIPTURE (NIV):
"My grace is sufficient for you, for my power is made perfect in weakness." — 2 Corinthians 12:9

PRAYER:
Lord, You know the places where I still struggle, and You love me there just as fully as everywhere else. Teach me to lay this burden in Your hands instead of trying to fight it in my own strength. Heal the places in me that hunger for comfort more than nourishment, and remind me that my worth is not measured, but atoned for through Your love. Help me walk in grace, not guilt, and trust You to finish what You have begun in me. Amen.

Now that we've gotten that out of the way, let's talk about the two recipes I do have that are healthy or at least semi-healthy. First, it's my Chocolate Ginger Muffins. My friend Myra said she actually "preferred" these over regular muffins! (See Myra's story in the Friends and Family section for the recipe)

The second healthy recipe is for Cinnamon Baked Apples. This is probably the only way I'll eat apples. Well, I'll also scarf down apple pie. Most fruits, except for bananas, don't excite me. The only way I'll eat them is if they're covered in sugar and butter and baked in a pie shell! As a matter of fact, when I get to Heaven, I'm going to find Eve and say you started the

downfall of mankind and got kicked out of the Garden of Eden over an apple? Really? Apple pie maybe, but a plain old apple?! I just can't wrap my head around that. But I do find it interesting that the "temptation" the devil used to get Adam and Eve to trip up and screw up their paradise was food. That gives me some comfort that I'm not the only one who found food just a bit too enticing at times. I share all of this for my friends who struggle with an eating disorder. I pray that you can turn it over to God and let Him rule your appetite and not your taste buds.

Cinnamon Baked Apples (or Peaches)

4 large apples
   (such as Honeycrisp or Fuji)
¼ cup walnuts, chopped
¼ cup rolled oats
2 Tbsp unsalted butter, softened
2 Tbsp brown sugar
2 Tbsp maple syrup
½ tsp ground cinnamon
¼ tsp ground nutmeg
1 pinch of salt
Vanilla ice cream or whipped
   cream (optional)

Start by coring the apples. Take that stem out of the middle. Easiest with an apple corer or you can carefully do it with a paring knife.

Next, preheat your oven to 350°F.

In a medium bowl, mix together the walnuts, oats, butter, brown sugar, maple syrup, cinnamon, nutmeg, and a pinch of salt. Stir until all the ingredients are well combined.

Next, stuff the apples. First, put them in your baking dish, then spoon the filling into each apple, pressing down gently to fill the cavity.

Transfer the baking dish to the oven and bake for 30 to 35 minutes, or until the apples are tender and the filling is golden brown. If you're cooking peaches, reduce the cooking time by ten minutes.

Note: If I'm really trying to avoid sugar, I will substitute Swerve Brown sugar instead of using real brown sugar. But heads up, any sugar substitute is not going to bake and react in the oven the way real sugar does. It just boils down to science and chemistry. There's just something about the makeup of nature's sugar that will always give you a better caramelization and taste than sugar made in a lab. But if you know that going in and don't expect the "sugar free' desserts to have the mouthfeel or texture, then you won't be so disappointed when eating the low calorie healthy dessert option.

Greek Yogurt Parfait with Honey-Almond Crunch

Parfait:
2 cups plain or vanilla Greek yogurt
   (can use nonfat or full-fat)
2 cups mixed berries
   (fresh or frozen strawberries,
   blueberries, raspberries)
2 Tbsp honey or pure maple syrup
1 tsp vanilla extract
Pinch of cinnamon (optional)

Crunch:
½ cup rolled oats
¼ cup sliced almonds
   (or chopped pecans/walnuts)
1 Tbsp honey
1 Tbsp coconut oil or olive oil
Pinch of sea salt

This delicious dessert can be changed up in many ways to accomodate your favorite fruits. Desserts don't have to be guilty pleasures, they can be reminders of how sweet God's gifts truly are. When we nourish our bodies with gratitude, every bite becomes a celebration of His goodness.

"Gracious words are a honeycomb, sweet to the soul and healing to the bones." —Proverbs 16:24

Devotion

Why is it that a candy bar tastes better than carrots? Or sleep feels better than exercise? Why do soft drinks taste better than water? We've trained our taste buds into thinking processed, sugar-fied, deep fried, and a side of fries makes up three square meals a day. Now let me be the first to say, I used to think only a man could make my knees go weak, but truly, the smell of fried dough, like donuts or a funnel cake, and I turn into a puddle in the middle of the floor! I still don't understand why they're not part of the food pyramid.

Here's my point: our diets affect everything we do. If we're not feeling good, we're not responding well to what Jesus has called us to do. Eating healthy will always be an uphill battle for me, but I want to remind myself that God is my sustenance for the long haul, not a chocolate-filled donut!

In the same way that our physical appetites can get conditioned toward what brings quick pleasure instead of real nourishment, our spiritual appetites can drift toward what is easy, shallow or entertaining instead of what truly feeds the soul. The body craves sugar, grease, and comfort food, while the spirit often craves comfort, distraction, and emotional "junk food," instead of truth. Just as a steady diet of donuts and fast food eventually weakens the body, a steady diet of easy inspiration without real Scripture, prayer, or discipline weakens the soul.

We rarely drift toward what is good for us without intention. You do not wake up one morning suddenly fit and full of energy because you once thought about eating a salad. Growth requires nourishment and consistency. The same is true with our walk with Christ. We cannot snack on His presence occasionally and expect the strength to run a marathon of faith. We need a steady diet of His Word, His voice, His presence, and His peace.

Accepting what God offers reaches us deeply. In that nourishment, He is strengthening us for the journey. So when your body or your spirit starts craving the quick fix, pause and ask what you are really hungry for. Is it temporary comfort, distraction, validation, or peace? Or is it time spent in the presence of the One who satisfies every longing in a lasting way?

SCRIPTURE:
"Jesus answered, It is written: Man shall not live on bread alone, but on every word that comes from the mouth of God." —Matthew 4:4

PRAYER:
Lord, teach my heart to hunger for what truly nourishes. Help me recognize when I am reaching for quick comfort instead of coming to You for real strength. When my spirit grows weak or distracted, draw me back to Your Word and Your presence. Give me the discipline to feed my soul with what lasts, not just what satisfies for a moment. Be my daily bread, my portion, and my sustaining strength. I want to live fueled by You, not by temporary fixes. In Jesus' name, Amen.

Cutting Techniques

CHOP

Rough, irregularly shaped pieces, typically similar in size, ensure even cooking. Ideal for soups, stews, stir-fries.

**EXAMPLE FOODS:
CARROTS, ZUCCHINI, POTATOES.**

DICE

Uniform, cube-shaped pieces are perfect for salsa, salads, casseroles, and sautés, ensuring consistency for enhanced cooking and presentation.

**EXAMPLE FOODS:
ONIONS, TOMATOES, ZUCCHINI, MANGOES.**

SLICE

Thin, flat pieces with uniform thickness, perfect for sandwiches, salads, garnishes, or layering in dishes like casseroles.

**EXAMPLE FOODS:
CUCUMBERS, ONIONS, TOMATOES, APPLES, ZUCCHINI.**

JULIENNE

Long, thin matchstick pieces, ideal for stir-fries, slaws, garnishes, or salads that call for a visually appealing presentation.

**EXAMPLE FOODS:
CARROTS, CUCUMBERS, BELL PEPPERS.**

BATONNET

Thick, long rectangular sticks, perfect for French fries, crudité platters, or pre-cut snacks.

**EXAMPLE FOODS:
POTATOES, CARROTS, ZUCCHINI.**

MINCE

Very fine, small, and irregular pieces, ideal for flavoring marinades, sauces, dressings, and seasoning blends, where ingredients need to seamlessly integrate.

**EXAMPLE FOODS:
GARLIC, GINGER, PARSLEY, CILANTRO.**

CHIFFONADE

Thin, ribbon-like strips created by rolling and slicing leafy greens, commonly used as garnishes for pasta, soups, or salads.

BRUNOISE

A very fine dice, perfect for garnishing soups, consommés, or dishes that require a refined, polished presentation.

BIAS CUT

Diagonal slices create more surface area than straight cuts, making them ideal for stir-fries, sautéed vegetables, and presentations.

Herbs Guide

SWEET HERBS

STEVIA

Intensely sweet; a natural sugar alternative for beverages and baked goods.

BASIL

Sweet and slightly peppery; a classic for Italian dishes and desserts.

MINT

Refreshing and sweet; perfect for teas, salads, and cocktails.

LEMON BALM

Bright and slightly sweet; used in teas and desserts.

SPICY HERBS

OREGANO

Bold and pungent; essential in Mediterranean and Mexican cuisines.

THYME

Robust and earthy; works well with meats and soups.

SAGE

Strong and slightly peppery; ideal for poultry and stuffing.

HORSERADISH

Pungent and spicy; used in sauces and pickles.

EARTHY HERBS

PARSLEY

Clean and grassy; a versatile garnish for any dish.

CILANTRO

Herbaceous with slight citrus undertones; common in curries and salsa.

DILL

Mildly tangy with earthy tones; pairs well with fish and potatoes.

SORREL

Earthy and slightly tart; great for soups and sauces.

CITRUSY HERBS

LEMONGRASS

Citrus-forward and fragrant; used in Asian cuisine.

LEMON BALM

Lemon-flavored with mild sweetness; perfect for teas and salads.

CILANTRO

Slight citrus notes; enhances salsas and curries.

LEMON VERBENA

Citrusy and aromatic; great for infusions and marinades.

SAVORY HERBS

ROSEMARY

Woody and earthy; ideal for roasted dishes and breads.

BAY LEAVES

Mildly aromatic and savory; perfect for soups and stews.

CHIVES

Mild onion flavor; excellent in salads, dips, and garnishes.

LOVAGE

Strong celery-like flavor; adds depth to broths and stews.

AROMATIC HERBS

LAVENDER

Floral with subtle sweetness; used in desserts and infusions.

CHAMOMILE

Mildly sweet and floral; popular in calming teas.

ROSE GERANIUM

Rosy and slightly minty; used in desserts and aromatic oils.

LEMON VERBENA

Delicate citrus and floral notes; lovely in teas and syrups.

Kitchen Conversions

1 Stick
1/2 Cup

1 Tbsp Fresh
1 TSspDry

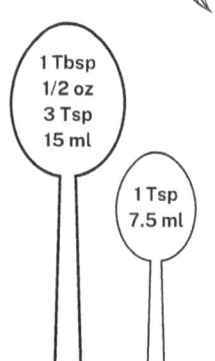

1 Tbsp
1/2 oz
3 Tsp
15 ml

1 Tsp
7.5 ml

A PINCH	1/16 tsp
A SMIDGE	1/32 tsp
A DASH	1/8 Dash

Liquid Measurements

OUNCE	TSP	TBSP	ML	CUP	PINT	QUART
1 oz	6 tsp	2 tbsp	30 ml	1/8 c	-	-
2 oz	12 tsp	4 tbsp	60 ml	1/4 c	-	-
2 2/3 oz	16 tsp	5 tbsp	80 ml	1/3 c	-	-
4 oz	24 tsp	8 tbsp	120 ml	1/2 c	-	-
5 1/3 oz	32 tsp	11 tbsp	160 ml	2/3 c	-	-
6 oz	36 tsp	12 tbsp	177 ml	3/4 c	-	-
8 oz	48 tsp	16 tbsp	240 ml	1 c	1/2 pt	1/4 pt
16 oz	96 tsp	32 tbsp	470 ml	2 c	1 p	1/2 p
32 oz	192 tsp	64 tbsp	950 ml	4 c	2 p	1 p

Dry Measurements

OUNCE	TBSP	CUP	GRAM	POUND
1/2 oz	1 tbsp	1/16 c	15 g	-
1 oz	2 tbsp	1/8 c	28 g	-
2 oz	4 tbsp	1/4 c	57 g	-
3 oz	6 tbsp	1/3 c	85 g	-
4 oz	8 tbsp	1/2 c	115 g	1/4 lb
8 oz	16 tbsp	1 c	227 g	1/2 lb
12 oz	24 tbsp	1 1/2 c	340 g	3/4 lb
16 oz	32 tbsp	2 c	455 g	1 lb

Soft - 5 min
Medium - 7 min
Hard - 9 min

145° F

145° F

165° F

145° F

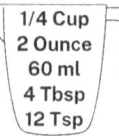

1/4 Cup
2 Ounce
60 ml
4 Tbsp
12 Tsp

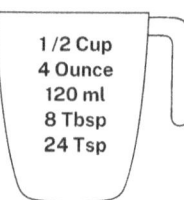

1/2 Cup
4 Ounce
120 ml
8 Tbsp
24 Tsp

1 Gallon
4 Quart
8 Pint
16 Cups
128 Ounces
3.8 Liters

1 Quart
2 Pint
4 Cups
32 Ounces
950 ml

1 Pint
2 Cups
16 Ounces
480 ml

OVEN TEMPERATURE

GAS	°F	°C
9	475	245
8	450	230
7	425	220
6	400	205
5	375	190
4	350	175
3	325	165
2	300	150
1	275	135
1/2	250	120

1 Cup
8 Ounce
240 ml
16 Tbsp
48 Tsp

Cooking Temperatures

Beef & Lamb

Blue Rare	110°F	43°C	Lightly seared, deep purple-red coloured
Rare	120°F-130°F	49°C-54°C	Deep red edge to edge
Medium Rare	130°F-135°F	54°C-57°C	Bright red centre, brown boarder
Medium	135°F-145°F	57°C-63°C	Pink centre
Medium Well	145°F-155°F	63°C-68°C	Almost no pink centre, mostly brown
Well	155°F- up	68°C- up	Brown all the way through
Ground Beef	160°F	71°C	Easy to pull apart, fork tender
Beef Bristket	190°F-250°F	86°C-96°C	

Pork

Medium	137°F	58°C	Some pink, juicy
USDA - Done	145°F	63°C	Cream coloured, firm
Well Done	150°F- up	66°C	Cream coloured, tough
Pre Cooked Ham	120°F	49°C	Caramelized, pink, juicy
Sausage	160°F	71°C	Warm, juicy
Pork Ribs - BBQ	190°F-205°F	88°C-96°C	Fall off the bone
Pork Shoulder - BBQ	190°F-205°F	88°C-96°C	Fork tender

Poultry

Whole or Ground	165°F	74°C	USDA & Chef recommended
Legs and Thighs	170-180°F	77°C-82°C	More tender at higher temps

Seafood

Ahi Tuna	115°F	46°C	Sashimi Grade
Shrimp	120°F	49°C	Pink, slightly constricted, tender
Salmon	125°F	52°C	Flaky and tender
Halibut	130°F	54°C	Opaque, moist
Scallops	130°F	54°C	Milky white, firm
Lobster & Crab	140°F	60°C	Opaque, not constricted

PRO TIPS:
Always remember when cooking meats the temperature can rise 10°F - 15°F when resting
Always let meats dethaw at room temp

Loaves, Fishes, & Last-Minute Fixes

These are ten tried-and-true tricks that'll keep supper on track and your house slippers right where they belong! On your feet!

Whether you're an experienced cook or a novice, taking the time to learn some of these lesser-known cooking tips can help you create delicious and impressive dishes. Read on to discover some surprising and unexpected cooking tips that can give you the edge in the kitchen.

1. Homemade Buttermilk
Just put 1 tbsp of lemon juice or white vinegar into one cup of whole milk. Let it sit 5 minutes.

2. Backyard BBQ Sauce
1 cup ketchup
¼ cup brown sugar
2 Tbsp apple cider vinegar
1 tbsp Worcestershire
½ tsp smoked paprika
    (if you're a LA girl you've got this on hand)
Simmer 10 minutes

3. Baking Powder Backup Plan
¼ tsp baking soda
½ tsp cream of tartar
¼ tsp cornstarch
Mix together for each teaspoon you need.

4. Breadcrumbs from Scratch
Toast two slices of bread (preferably stale), crumble them. I put them in my food processor. Add Italian seasoning.

5. Brown Sugar Emergency Fix
If you're out of brown sugar (or yours turned into a brick), Mix 1 cup white sugar with 1 tbsp of molasses (2 tbsp for dark brown) using a fork or the paddle attachment of your stand mixer.

6. Make-Do "Cream"
Melt ¼ cup butter and stir it into ¾ cup milk. It won't whip, but it'll thicken up your soup or sauce just fine.

7. DIY Lemon Zest (If You Don't Have Lemons)
When you need lemon zest but have no lemons, combine a few drops of lemon extract with a teaspoon of sugar. And if you have oranges, the zest of the orange gives you that bright citrus flavor as well.

8. Ranch Mix in a Minute
1 Tbsp of parsley
1 tsp each of dill, garlic powder, onion powder
1/2 tsp salt
½ tsp pepper
Stir it into mayo or sour cream and you've got ranch that'll make you swear off store-bought forever.

9. Quick Marinade Magic
¼ cup Soy sauce
2 tbsp olive oil
2 tbsp brown sugar
splash of vinegar
Whisk together.
Perfect for chicken, pork, or vegetables that need a little personality.

10. Self-Rising Flour Switcheroo
For when you're elbow-deep in biscuit dough and realize it's all-purpose, not self-rising:
1 cup all purpose flour
1 ½ tsp baking powder
¼ tsp salt
Give it a stir and carry on like nothing happened.

Closing

Well, I hope you've enjoyed my little culinary journey. How I went from Tallulah tomboy to a baking, cooking, cookie decorating diva (not diva in the conceited sense but someone who has somewhat mastered their kitchen craft! Lol)

I often say the kitchen is my playground. Thank you, April, for letting me steal that! It's my therapy. I enjoy the process of creating a meal. Heck, I even enjoy the cleanup! Yep, there's something so satisfying about cleaning up and clearing out all the messed-up pots, pans and paraphernalia that went in to creating a great dish.

I often think God does the same for us. He sees us chop, slice, dice and stir up our lives until it looks like one big ole mess. But when some heat is applied, you'll finally end up with a dessert or delicacy ready to be enjoyed. And when the last bite is taken, the dirty dishes are washed and put away, then there's a clean slate for God's next delicious experience.

A good reminder, whether that meal (experience) was divine or disappointing, and who hasn't burned something in the kitchen every once in a while, we get a chance to start again. Start fresh. New ingredients mixed with some foundational staples, and the next adventure begins. Either way, God says, "Taste and see that I am good." Jesus didn't die for you so that you could just survive this life here on earth. He came so that you might have it more abundantly.

I'm praying that from this day forward you will savor each moment on this earth by spending time in the best 'recipes for life' book ever written, the Bible, and with the "Bread of Life", Jesus.

Jesus said to them, "I am the bread of life; whoever comes to me shall not hunger, and whoever believes in me shall never thirst. –John 6:35 ESV

Make every day delicious my friend!

—Tammi

Devotion

Many of us grow up hearing that God loves us, but it is not until we slow down long enough to sit in His presence that we begin to feel it. The world trains us to believe love must be earned through success, in our performance, or by doing everything right. But the Lord's love does the opposite: it quiets striving, silences shame, and invites us simply to be held.

Closeness with God doesn't come from trying harder; it comes from turning toward Him. Just a whisper of "Lord, I'm here" is enough to open the door for His peace to meet us. He is not waiting for a polished, perfect week of spiritual discipline. He is waiting for your heart. You do not get closer to Him by climbing up, you come closer by slowing down.

God doesn't love you because of anything, He loves you before everything. Before the mistake, the victory, or the season you're in today. His love already had your name on it.

When you finally realize you don't have to strive for His affection, you begin to live from a place of deep security. You stop questioning whether you are enough and start trusting that He already is.

SCRIPTURE (NIV):
"The Lord your God is with you, the Mighty Warrior who saves. He will take great delight in you; in His love He will no longer rebuke you, but will rejoice over you with singing." — Zephaniah 3:17

PRAYER:
Father, help me rest in the truth of Your unfailing love. Teach me to lean instead into Your heart, where I am already known and cherished. Let my life be rooted in Your presence, and let closeness with You become my greatest joy. Amen.

MICHTER HOUSE
PUBLISHING
an imprint of
Rope Swing Publishing